WHO
NEEDS
A
COOKBOOK

Also by Arthur Hawkins

THE STEAK BOOK

WHO NEEDS A COOKBOOK

how to make 222 delicious international
dishes with a minimum of direction

by

ARTHUR HAWKINS

PRENTICE-HALL, INC., ENGLEWOOD CLIFFS, N. J.

Who Needs a Cookbook, by Arthur Hawkins

© 1968 by Arthur Hawkins

Library of Congress Catalog Card Number: 68-27800
Printed in the United States of America · T

Prentice-Hall International, Inc., London
Prentice-Hall of Australia, Pty. Ltd., Sydney
Prentice-Hall of Canada, Ltd., Toronto
Prentice-Hall of India Private Ltd., New Delhi
Prentice-Hall of Japan, Inc., Tokyo

To Helen

FOREWORD

In 1678 William Penn came across a recently published "cookery" book. So impressed was he that he sat down and wrote what amounts to a review of the book. He wrote: This book is so complete and so full of fine instructions for preparing food of all kinds that there seems no reason for writing another book on cookery.

If you find no quotes around William Penn's utterance, it is because I doubt whether his exact words can be reconstructed, and who would dare put words into the mouth of this sterling Quaker? Let it rest that Mr. Penn did make such a remark about a "cookery" book published three hundred years ago.

But wouldn't you like to have the privilege of seeing the color of Mr. Penn's face if he walked into one of today's bookstores and took a gander at the cookery shelves?

Today you can find books written in English on the cooking of almost any foreign country. There are books on German cooking, Chinese, Japanese, Irish, Mexican, Spanish, and Swiss; Armenian, Russian, Polish, and Hungarian; Polynesian, Dutch, and Greek. There are dozens of books on French cooking—and Italian.

American cooking? What kind? There's New England, New Orleans, and New York cooking; Southern cooking, Western cooking. And there's a cookbook for just about any of the fifty states.

You want a Jewish cookbook—we've got it. A Catholic, Moslem, Zen, and Baptist cookbook, too.

And there are cookbooks for those unfortunate people who are lacking in the proper cooking equipment; for those who have only a casserole or a blender or a chafing dish or a freezer.

There are cookbooks for people who live on a limited diet— eat only eggs, only desserts, only salads, or only steak. Or for people who like to eat everything but would rather count calories.

And there are cookbooks for people who are in love with the idea of cooking (because it brings them great joy) and for those who hate it.

All these books give you exact instructions for mixing together exact amounts of ingredients which have to be cooked in a very special manner for a prescribed length of time at x degrees Fahrenheit. If you follow the recipe meticulously and serve the resulting dish properly with just the right sauce, your guests will smack their lips with satisfaction and throw you kisses.

But what if, just as you are about to slide the casserole into the 273½-degree oven, you discover that you have only half a bay leaf, not enough tomato paste, and no shallots at all. The dish is ruined?

Not with this cookbook!

This is a cookbook that shrugs off the little ordinary frailties of forgetfulness, neglect, or error and shows you how to get around them.

8

In this book you will find a selection of recipes for famous and unusual dishes of many nations written with a minimum of fussy cookbookish details, but resulting in a maximum of gastronomic satisfaction. (Who needs a Chinese cookbook to cook Chinese, or a Hungarian cookbook for goulash!)

So tie on your apron, don your chef's hat, reach for a skillet, and get going. Experience the freedom of creative cooking without a cookbook looking over your shoulder at every move.

CONTENTS

WHO
NEEDS
A
COOKBOOK

1

WHO
NEEDS
A
HUNGARIAN
COOKBOOK

WHO NEEDS A HUNGARIAN COOKBOOK

TÖLTÖTT TOJÁS (*Stuffed Eggs, Hungarian Style*)

MUSHROOMS À LA SAVARIN

KÁPOSZTALEVES (*Sauerkraut Soup*)

HALÁSZLÉ (*Fisherman's Soup*)

CHICKEN PAPRIKA

HUNGARIAN ROAST VEAL (OR BEEF)

GULYÁS (*Hungarian Goulash*)

PAPRIKASH

BORJÚPAPRIKÁS (*Paprika Schnitzel*)

HUNGARIAN COFFEE CAKE

CHEESECAKE

14

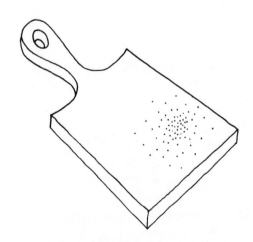

The food of Hungary is characterized by the almost constant use of paprika, the frequent use of sour cream, and the ever present cakes and pastries. Take all the liberties your conscience allows with all the other ingredients, but to cook Hungarian you'll almost certainly have to have paprika and/or sour cream. Maybe you didn't know it, but paprika comes in many delicious flavors ranging all the way from the very sweet to the very hot. In Hungary, where they grow a lot of the stuff (they do in Spain, too) there are five distinct grades: Noble-sweet, Semisweet, Rose (first grade), Strong (second grade), and Commercial (third grade).

Those Hungarian chefs who work hard at their trade often mix their paprikas to attain a distinctive flavor. Incidentally, paprika retains its beautiful red color best when added to hot fat or oil, rather than to water.

TÖLTÖTT TOJÁS (*Stuffed Eggs, Hungarian Style*)

Great to take along on a Hungarian picnic. If you're nowhere near Hungary and still want to go picnicking, just leave out the paprika. This recipe uses a dozen eggs, but who knows how many you want. If you only need eleven, get out your computer and calculate eleven-twelfths of all the ingredients. Or take a chance . . . guess!

12 hard-cooked eggs	shell the eggs and halve them lengthwise
3 tablespoons mayonnaise or salad dressing	remove the yolks and save the whites
2 tablespoons sour cream	in a bowl mash the yolks with all the other ingredients
2 scallions, finely chopped	
dash Worcestershire	put this mixture back into the whites and sprinkle with paprika
cayenne	
salt and pepper	
paprika	

15

MUSHROOMS À LA SAVARIN

Brillat-Savarin was a French lawyer and writer who lived in the late eighteenth and early nineteenth centuries. There is a story that he defended in court a chef who killed his wife's lover by serving him a dish of poison mushrooms. But there is no truth in it ... in fact, there really isn't such a story. I wonder how he got a mushroom dish named after him. I wonder how this mushroom dish got in the Hungarian chapter.

1 cup sliced mushrooms	brown the mushrooms and onions in butter and season to taste
1 medium onion, minced	
couple tablespoons butter	pour in the broth and simmer slowly until the mushrooms are tender
salt	
cayenne	stir in the flour-water mixture to thicken
½ cup beef broth	
tablespoon flour mixed with water	whip the cream a little, add to the mushrooms, and simmer a little, do not boil
½ cup sour cream	spoon onto the toast, sprinkle with paprika, and serve as canapés
toast points	
paprika	(serves about 4)

16

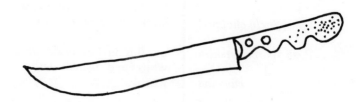

KÁPOSZTALEVES (*Sauerkraut Soup*)

This Hungarian soup is rich and hearty. It is recommended as a meal in itself. Serve it with great hunks of Italian or French bread and you won't need anything else. There's no need to follow this recipe exactly to produce a delicious soup. Just use your own judgment, but if you don't have a can of sauerkraut, it won't be Sauerkraut Soup. And if you don't have sour cream and paprika, it won't be Hungarian.

1 pound lean pork	put the meat, vegetables, and seasonings into a quart or so of water and boil for an hour or so
4 slices bacon	
1 ham hock (or something similar)	strain, cut the meat into cubes, and put back into the liquid with the vegetables
1 onion, sliced	
1 clove garlic, chopped	simmer for a half hour longer. mix flour with sour cream and add to the soup
1 green pepper, chopped	
1 tomato, sliced (or 1 tablespoon tomato paste)	heat without boiling. if you have some frankfurters or other sausage, slice them and add to the soup. serve hot
1 teaspoon each salt, pepper, paprika	
few caraway seeds	(serves about 6)
2 quarts water	
1 large can sauerkraut	
½ pint sour cream	
1 tablespoon flour	

17

HALÁSZLÉ (*Fisherman's Soup*)

Who ever heard of a Hungarian fisherman? And where would he fish in this landlocked country? Anyway, here is a fisherman's soup. It's Hungarian. It's good—and it's guaranteed! You can do almost anything you want to this soup and it will gain you compliments. I have listed possible ingredients to use, but if you don't have them on hand, improvise.

2 pounds some kind of fish bones and odds and ends

cook all the ingredients except last two about an hour

1 cup fresh celery, chopped

strain, keeping only the stock

1 cup fresh carrots, sliced

an onion or two, sliced

add the fish fillets, cut into pieces, and whatever vegetables you have

2 cloves garlic, chopped

simmer until tender, season to taste with any kind of seasoning

2 tablespoons fresh parsley

small piece ginger, if you have it

(serves about 6)

a teaspoon each pepper, salt, paprika

2 quarts water

a couple pounds some kind of fish fillets

18

fresh vegetables (any kind)

CHICKEN PAPRIKA

Here's a dish from Transylvania where vampires roam about at night. You can protect yourself from them by wearing a string of garlic around your neck, but a better idea is to take a chance on the vampires and use the garlic to cook up a pot of Chicken Paprika. If you suddenly discover you're all out of chicken, and it's dark out there, use veal or rabbit or squirrel, but for heaven's sake never use vampire.

2 broilers, quartered

flour

salt, pepper

2 tablespoons butter

2 onions, minced

2 cloves garlic, crushed

1 tomato, peeled and chopped

1 green pepper, minced

3 tablespoons paprika

1 tablespoon tomato paste

1 cup chicken stock

1 cup sour cream

dredge the chicken pieces in flour, season with salt and pepper, and sauté in butter until golden

add the onions, garlic, tomato, paprika, tomato paste, pepper, and stock. cover and continue cooking for a half hour or so

just before serving add the sour cream and heat without boiling

(serves 4)

19

HUNGARIAN ROAST VEAL (OR BEEF)

4 pounds veal roast or top round of beef	marinate the meat in the wine, oil and lemon juice, onion and garlic for a couple of hours
1 cup dry red wine	
2 tablespoons olive oil	trim off all the fat and skin and season with salt, pepper, cayenne, thyme, and paprika
the juice of 1 lemon	
1 onion, chopped	place in roasting pan, cover with strips of bacon, pour on the marinade, and cover with sour cream
1 clove garlic, minced	
salt, pepper	
cayenne	heat the oil and pour on top. sprinkle lavishly with paprika
thyme	cover and roast in a medium oven for a couple of hours. then uncover, turn up the heat, and brown
teaspoon paprika	
about 4 slices bacon	
4 tablespoons sour cream	serve with the pan gravy
½ cup oil	(serves 6 or 8)
paprika	

20

GULYÁS (*Hungarian Goulash*)

Here is one of the fine dishes of Central Europe. Princes have been known to resist the advances of beautiful women until after the goulash was served and consumed. The culinary success of master chefs in Hungary often rests on the ability to put together a superior goulash. A bachelor friend of mine who fancied him-self a pretty good cook wished to impress a certain young lady. He selected a recipe for goulash from his shelf of cookbooks to turn the trick. Carefully he stocked all the listed ingredients. When the important evening arrived, he set to work. He meticulously followed all the cooking directions set forth in his cookbook only to discover, after he had set the table, lit the candles, and poured wine, that he had no noodles on which to serve his creation. The young lady never tasted the goulash; my friend shot himself.

I was able to salvage the recipe from my friend's effects, and I offer it herewith for your delight. But a word of caution, please: If you find yourself without noodles, don't reach for a gun, use spaghetti or macaroni or even toast. And if you don't have pork on hand, use beef or veal—or both. You could even do without paprika. Of course it wouldn't be goulash, but it would be good!

2 pounds lean pork (or beef), diced

1 tablespoon flour

put the meat, flour, salt, paprika, and cayenne into a paper bag and shake until the meat is well coated

1 teaspoon salt (you may need more)

1 teaspoon paprika

couple dashes cayenne

put the oil, onions, garlic, peppers, and tomato into a heavy skillet and heat carefully. add the meat and sauté until golden brown

2 tablespoons olive oil (or whatever oil you have)

1 onion, chopped

add a little water (or dry red wine, if you wish) and simmer about a half hour or until tender

1 clove garlic, chopped

add the sour cream, cover and simmer again about 10 minutes

21

1 green pepper, chopped

1 teaspoon tomato paste (or a chopped tomato)

serve on hot noodles (or spaghetti or macaroni or toast or by itself)

1 pint sour cream (or you could use sweet cream and a little lemon juice)

(serves 4, maybe 6)

PAPRIKASH

This is an old Hungarian standby. You can make it almost any way you want, very hot or very sweet. Use one of the less tender cuts of beef, or if you have some pork hanging around, use that. Or use veal. To serve 6¾ people follow this recipe strictly. If you don't happen to have 6¾ people, call in a mathematician—or guess.

3 pounds some kind of beef, or veal or pork, cut into thin 1½-inch pieces

sear the meat slices on all sides in the oil. add the onion, garlic, tomato, and pepper

3 tablespoons olive oil, or what have you

cover and cook slowly about 2 hours. add a little water if necessary to prevent sticking

1 large onion, minced

1 clove garlic, crushed

stir in the paprika and continue cooking. add more water to make enough gravy. season to taste and garnish with pepper rings

1 tomato, chopped

1 green pepper, chopped

water

(serves 6¾)

1 tablespoon paprika

salt, pepper

green pepper rings

22

BORJÚPAPRIKÁS (*Paprika Schnitzel*)

A schnitzel is a thin slice of veal, pounded still thinner to about ⅛ inch thick. The Germans, Hungarians, Austrians, and Bavarians eat schnitzels all the time. (The Italians eat scallopini.) To be good, the schnitzel has to be young veal, free from gristle, membrane, or fat. If you start with first-rate meat, it's pretty hard to end up with a second-rate schnitzel.

couple pounds veal, sliced thin and pounded to ⅛ inch thick (or use pork or beef)

sauté the meat in the oil until brown and tender, and put on a warm platter

couple tablespoons oil

couple tablespoons minced onion

add the onion and bacon to the skillet and simmer a little, and season to taste

several slices bacon, chopped

salt, pepper

add the tomato paste and cream, and continue to simmer about 15 minutes

paprika

pour the sauce over the schnitzels and decorate with a little parsley

couple tablespoons tomato paste

(serves 4, maybe 6)

cup sour cream, of course

minced parsley

23

HUNGARIAN COFFEE CAKE

1 cup flour, sifted	mix the flour, milk, sugar, and yeast and beat well. put in a warm place for a couple hours to rise
1 cup warm milk	
4 tablespoons sugar	
2 packages (or cakes) yeast	meanwhile, cream the butter, egg yolks, and 5 tablespoons sugar. season with salt and add 3 cups flour and a cup of warm sour cream. mix thoroughly
½ pound butter	
6 egg yolks	
5 tablespoons sugar	add the yeast mixture and beat well with a wooden spoon
salt	
3 cups flour, sifted	beat the egg whites and fold them into the batter
1 cup warm sour cream	
6 egg whites	put about a third of the batter into a well-greased, floured cake pan and sprinkle with raisins, cinnamon, and nuts
raisins	
tablespoon cinnamon	pour on another third of the batter and sprinkle again with raisins, cinnamon, and nuts
chopped nuts (any kind)	
1 egg, beaten	put it into a warm place and let it rise for about a half hour. brush with beaten egg and bake in a 450° oven for 15 minutes. then cover with foil or oiled paper, turn the oven down (to about 350°), and bake an hour longer
powdered sugar	

remove from the pan and sprinkle with powdered sugar

(serves 4–6)

24

CHEESECAKE

Cheesecake is pretty universal stuff—both the kind you look at and the kind you eat. It is generally conceded that the latter variety had its origin in Hungary. It's not certain whether the recipe that follows is genuinely Hungarian, but it's a good one and it's easy!

4 small packages cream cheese (or 2 large)	blend the cheese, eggs, sugar, and ½ teaspoon vanilla
2 eggs	spoon the mixture into a well-buttered and floured cake pan. bake for 20 minutes at about 375°
½ cup sugar	
½ teaspoon vanilla	
butter	meanwhile, mix the sour cream, 2 tablespoons sugar, and ½ teaspoon vanilla
flour	
1½ cups sour cream	spread this mixture over the cake and bake 5 minutes longer
2 tablespoons sugar	
½ teaspoon vanilla	serve cold
	(serves 4–6)

25

2

WHO

NEEDS

A

FRENCH

COOKBOOK

WHO NEEDS A FRENCH COOKBOOK

CROQUE MONSIEUR (*Mr. Crunch*)

QUICHE LORRAINE (*Cheese and Bacon Tart*)

SOUPE À L'OIGNON (*Onion Soup*)

POTAGE PARMENTIER (*Potato and Leek Soup*)

VICHYSSOISE

POTAGE AU CRESSON (*Watercress Soup*)

TRUITE AU BLEU (*Blue Trout*)

BOUILLABAISSE

ESCARGOTS BOURGUIGNONNE (*Burgundy Snails*)

FILETS DE SOLE OU QU'AVEZ-VOUS
(*Fillets of Sole or What Have You*)

FILETS DE SOLE BERCY

FILETS DE SOLE BONNE FEMME

FILETS DE SOLE MARGUERY

ETC.

LE POULET MARENGO (*Chicken Marengo*)

STEAK AU POIVRE (*Steak with Pepper*)

BLANQUETTE DE VEAU (*White Veal Stew*)

BOEUF À LA BOURGUIGNONNE (*Beef, Burgundy Style*)

COEUR À LA CRÈME (*Cream Cheese Hearts*)

CRÊPES SUZETTE

CRÊPES (*French Pancakes*)

PÊCHES MELBA (*Peaches Melba*)

28

To the French, eating is the number-one pastime (well, almost), and they're very particular about what they eat and how it is prepared. So you can wander about the streets of Paris (any street) or of Marseilles (or of any city) or of any provincial town, drop into a restaurant (any restaurant, great or obscure), and be assured of getting good food.

The French love to eat and therefore they love to cook. So France is full of cookbooks? Not at all. Who needs a cookbook when you have a well-developed instinct for good eating—an instinct that tells you that snails are good to eat, and frogs' legs, overripe cheese, truffles, and tripe. Who needs a cookbook to spell out directions for preparing such wonderful foods.

The dishes that appear in this chapter, many of them classics that have withstood the test of years, vary so from province to province, from restaurant to restaurant, that you inevitably become aware of the creativity and personality of the chef in charge.

So, use your personality—create!

CROQUE MONSIEUR (*Mr. Crunch*)

8 thin slices bread	spread 4 slices of bread with butter and cover with Gruyère, ham, and Roquefort slices
butter	
4 thin slices Gruyère cheese	
4 thin slices ham	close the sandwiches with the other 4 slices of bread and cut into 16 canapés
4 thin slices Roquefort cheese	
1 egg	beat the egg and milk, dip the canapés, and sauté on both sides in butter until golden, crisp, and crunchy (*croque:* crunch)
2 tablespoons milk	

29

QUICHE LORRAINE *(Cheese and Bacon Tart)*

1 cup flour	make a soft pastry dough by mixing together a cup of flour, an egg yolk, ½ cup butter, and a pinch of salt. chill for a half hour and roll out into a thin pie shell on a floured board. place in a 9-inch pie pan and trim the edges. cover with waxed paper and bake in a preheated 400° oven for 10 minutes and remove from the oven
1 egg yolk	
½ cup butter	
pinch salt	
½ pound sliced bacon	
1½ cups grated or diced Gruyère cheese	
4 eggs	fry bacon until crisp, drain, crumble into bits, sprinkle onto the partially baked pie shell, and then add the cheese
2 cups heavy cream	
¼ teaspoon salt	lightly beat the eggs with the cream and seasonings and pour into the pie shell
¼ teaspoon dry mustard	
dash nutmeg	bake in a moderate oven (325°) for about half an hour or until golden and center is firm. serve warm. cut into 12 slices for canapés or 6 for a luncheon dish
dash cayenne	

30

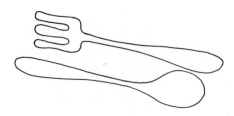

France is very probably the birthplace of modern soups. The pot on the back of the stove was the receptacle for leftover bits of meat, fowl, and vegetables, gravies and sauces. The wonderful essence that evolved became the basic stock from which an endless variety of soups were—and still are—made.

SOUPE À L'OIGNON (*Onion Soup*)

Throw into the basic stock a few onions and a little cheese (plentiful staples of France) and you have the nation's number-one soup.

Recipes for making onion soup vary all over France, so how can you go wrong? Here's one to try for a starter—vary it as you wish.

thinly sliced onions (3 cups for 4 servings)

4 tablespoons butter and/or oil

in a saucepan sauté the onions in the butter-oil until golden, sprinkle in the flour, salt and pepper and sugar. simmer—stir

1 tablespoon flour

½ teaspoon salt

pour in the beef stock and simmer 15 minutes longer

add the wine and check the seasoning

pepper (freshly ground is best)

dash sugar

1 quart beef stock or bouillon

½ cup dry white wine or dry Vermouth (or leave it out)

sprinkle toast with grated cheese, place in bottom of four crocks, pour in the soup, cover with cheese, and place under the broiler until the cheese melts and forms a brown crust

4 slices French bread, toasted

½ cup grated cheese (Parmesan, Swiss, or Gruyère)

31

POTAGE PARMENTIER *(Potato and Leek Soup)*

Here's another great soup of France. It's delicious, it's versatile, it's foolproof. You don't need a cookbook—all you need is potatoes and leeks. (Of course, a little water won't hurt and a little salt will help.)

All you do is simmer the potatoes (3 or 4 cups, peeled—of course—and sliced) and the leeks (3 or 4 cups, including the tender tops, sliced) in a couple of quarts of water and add a tablespoon of salt. When the vegetables are good and soft, put the soup through a food mill, blender, or soup strainer and there you are with enough potage for 6 or 7 people.

If you're fresh out of leeks, use onions or scallions (small cousins of leeks). If you want to get fancy, stir in about ½ cup cream or a couple tablespoons butter and decorate with chopped chives or parsley.

VICHYSSOISE

This is an American invention (the French like it, too), created by Louis Diat, a great French chef operating in New York where it gets pretty hot in the summer. To make it you blend chicken stock or canned chicken broth with basic potato-leek soup and serve chilled.

POTAGE AU CRESSON *(Watercress Soup)*

Follow the potato-leek soup recipe, adding a cup of fresh watercress (chopped and with stems removed) to the potatoes and leeks. Then after putting it all through a food mill, add a little cream and chicken stock (if you wish), and *voilà* you have Potage au Cresson—a great soup!

OTHER VARIATIONS

To the potato-leek base add at the start a cup or so of the follow-
ing ingredients, then simmer, strain, season, and serve:
Sliced carrots, turnips, or mushrooms.
Strained canned tomatoes.
Leftover beans, peas, or lentils.
Cauliflower, broccoli, okra, zucchini, or cucumbers.
Lettuce, spinach, kale, cabbage, or celery.

Or mix in two or three vegetables, add chopped ham or bacon.
Vary the seasoning: add a small pinch of saffron, a bit of curry,
a little chili powder or paprika, a touch of garlic.

Be adventurous—be the first cook on your block to serve choco-
late-leek soup (it might be good, at that)!

TRUITE AU BLEU (*Blue Trout*)

This is a rare and sensational dish, rare because only freshly
caught fish can be used and sensational because it really is a
vivid blue in color. Truite au Bleu is served in country inns
throughout France where trout abound.

equal parts water and wine vinegar	make a court bouillon of all the ingredients in an enamel pot (always keep acids away from aluminum pots) and simmer for a half hour and strain off the solids
chopped onions	
parsley	
thyme	catch the trout, degut but do not scale or wash, toss them into the court bouillon, and poach for 4 or 5 minutes.
a bay leaf	
salt	remove the now blue trout and serve hot with melted butter or cold with Hollandaise or mayonnaise
freshly ground pepper	
freshly caught trout	

33

BOUILLABAISSE

Bouillabaisse first happened in Marseilles and was composed of seafood indigenous to the region: sole, brill, roach (not the kind found in kitchens), turbot, dace, racasse (Mediterranean hogfish). You haven't got these fish and so you can't make Bouillabaisse? Nonsense, what's wrong with lobster and eel, and shrimp, and red snapper?

You don't need Marseilles—you don't need a cookbook. Go to the fish store and pick out a variety of fish, shellfish, and mollusks, put them in a pot with some seasonings, a little wine, and a pinch of saffron, and turn on the heat. You'll get what Thackeray called "a noble dish—a sort of soup, or broth, or brew—a hotch-potch of all sorts of fishes." What more could you ask for? Guidance? Then try this recipe:

olive oil (½ cup or so)

in a large pot heat the oil, toss in the garlic, onions, thyme, bay leaf, and fennel, and cook for 5 minutes

crushed garlic (2 or 3 cloves)

2 or 3 onions, chopped

½ teaspoon thyme

add the tomatoes, clam juice, wine, and saffron and cook 10 minutes longer

½ bay leaf

½ teaspoon crushed fennel

throw in the cut-up seafood (clams, if any, should go in last to keep them tender) and boil quickly at high heat for 10 minutes. (the high heat blends the oil with the water juices and the 10 minutes cooks the fish without softening them)

2 cups tomatoes, chopped

34

1 cup bottled clam juice

1 cup dry white wine

1 pinch saffron

serve in bowls with chunks of French bread

1 lobster, cut into pieces and with claw cracked (or use rock lobster tail)

(serves 6)

1 dozen mussels or small clams, scrubbed, or both

*1 dozen raw shrimp, shelled
and deveined, or scallops
or both*

*1 pound cod or haddock, or
red snapper or eel or whiting,
cleaned and cut into pieces*

ESCARGOTS BOURGUIGNONNE (*Burgundy Snails*)

Snails come in shells? They come in cans, too, with the shells packaged separately. And that's why you can serve snails right in your own home that are just as good as those in Burgundy— well, almost.

*½ pound butter
(sweet butter is best)*

in a mixing bowl cream the butter, shallots, garlic, parsley, and condiments until you have a smooth green paste

*1 tablespoon finely chopped
shallots (or scallions)*

1 clove garlic, crushed

wash and drain the snails according to directions on the can

*1 tablespoon finely chopped
parsley*

a little salt

scrub the shells and put a little of the snail butter in the bottom of each. shove in the snails and fill with more of the butter

dash pepper

2 dozen snails

place shells into a pie pan, open side up, and bake in a 400° oven for about 10 minutes

2 dozen snail shells

serve hot with snail forks (or cocktail forks) and with hunks of French bread to mop up the sauce

35

FILETS DE SOLE OU QU'AVEZ-VOUS
(Fillets of Sole or What Have You)

Sole swim in European waters and seldom get as far as the United States unless they get here by air.

What we call sole—lemon sole or gray sole—are flounder, fluke, or plaice or (in the Pacific) brill.

The French, who know a good thing when they taste it, often debone the sole and poach it in wine. Add sweet butter and shallots and you can call it Filets de Sole Bercy. You can do the same with flounder, fresh water trout, weakfish, pompano, or any close-grained, delicately flavored fish.

FILETS DE SOLE BERCY

1 tablespoon finely minced shallots (or scallions)

butter a shallow 10- or 12-inch baking dish and sprinkle half the shallots in the bottom

1½ pounds clean fish fillets cut into serving pieces

salt and pepper

salt and pepper the fish fillets, place them into the dish, sprinkle with remaining shallots, dot with butter, and cover with wine and fish stock

2 tablespoons butter (sweet, if you have it)

36

½ cup dry white wine or dry Vermouth

¼ cup fish stock or bottled clam juice

cover with a piece of waxed paper and simmer in a preheated 425° oven about 5 minutes, remove the paper, baste with the sauce in the dish, and resume cooking until fork pierces the fish easily. do not overcook

(serves 4)

FILETS DE SOLE BONNE FEMME

Make a sauce by adding a flour-butter paste and a little cream to the poaching liquid in the Bercy recipe. Add a cup of sliced fresh mushrooms that have been sautéed in butter. Pour the sauce over the poached fillets (add Hollandaise sauce, if you wish), brown under the broiler, and garnish with chopped parsley or tarragon.

FILETS DE SOLE MARGUERY

Add shrimp and mussels that have been sautéed in butter with *fines herbes* to Filets de Sole Bercy and brown as usual.

ETC.

Be your own French chef. To the poaching liquid obtained in the Bercy recipe add ingredients of your own choosing: grated cheese, cream, sliced grapes, truffles (if you just happen to have some around), oysters, scallops, tomato paste, garlic, crisp bacon bits.

For variety, try serving the fillets folded or rolled with stuffings inside.

Give your creation a name, if you wish, or just eat it and enjoy it.

37

LE POULET MARENGO *(Chicken Marengo)*

Napoleon fought the battle of Marengo. He won it. Meanwhile, his chef was fighting the battle of food shortages. Chickens and onions and tomatoes and garlic he had—but no butter! *Sacrebleu!*

The chef sneaked in some oil instead and fried the chickens in it. Then he threw in a few eggs and fried them, added a few garnishes, and fearfully placed the unheard-of concoction before the hungry general. Napoleon removed his hand from his coat, sampled the dish, and smiled. *Vive la France!*

No butter? Use oil. No chicken? Use pheasant—or swan. No mushrooms? Use cepes. No bread? Let them eat cake! If the French can run in these substitutions, why can't you?

Start with the Marengo recipe that follows and let your conscience be your guide. For example, throw in some olives—and/or shrimp—and/or fried eggs.

Or use red wine instead of white, toss in a little chopped ham, or bacon, some thyme, a bay leaf, and flambé with cognac. *Voilà*—now you have Le Coq au Vin!

38

1 4-pound stewing chicken, cut into serving pieces	dredge the chicken with flour, salt and pepper, until well coated
flour	
salt and pepper	cook in hot oil until golden brown on all sides, using a heavy saucepan
3 tablespoons oil	
1 can tomatoes	add the tomatoes, tomato paste, wine, stock, and garlic. simmer for about an hour
1 tablespoon tomato paste	
½ cup dry white wine	add the onions and mushrooms and continue cooking for a half hour longer or until chicken is tender
½ cup stock (chicken or veal) or bouillon	

1 whole clove garlic

12 small onions

12 small mushrooms

croutons

chopped parsley

place the chicken pieces into a hot serving dish, garnish with the mushrooms and onions, pour the sauce over them, sprinkle with croutons of fried bread and parsley

(serves 4)

STEAK AU POIVRE *(Steak with Pepper)*

2½ pounds good, tender steak, 1½ inches thick

salt

3 tablespoons whole black pepper

¼ cup olive oil

¼ cup brandy (or whiskey)

½ pint cream

chopped parsley

trim excess fat from steak. remove the bone and season with salt on both sides

crush the peppercorns coarsely (put them in a towel and sock them with the bottom of a skillet) and pound them into the steak until both sides are heavily coated

broil on both sides in a very hot oiled skillet. remove onto a heated platter and place in a warm oven

pour off all but 1 tablespoon of the oil and drippings, add the brandy, flame for about a minute, and add the cream. heat—stir

when sauce thickens pour it over the steak and garnish with chopped parsley

(serves 4)

39

BLANQUETTE DE VEAU *(White Veal Stew)*

This is one of the oldest French dishes known to man. And here is the authentic recipe passed down from mouth to mouth. It's a bit of a workout but well worth it. You'll see.

2½ pounds shoulder, leg, or breast of veal, cut into 2-inch cubes	parboil the veal in a quart of salted water, using a heavy saucepan. skim the scum
1 quart water	when scum has stopped foaming, put in the onion, carrot, celery, herbs, and peppercorns, cover and simmer for an hour or until meat is tender
almost a tablespoon salt	
1 large onion, stuck with a clove	
5 tablespoons chopped carrot	boil the mushrooms in a little water for a few minutes and cook the onions in 2 tablespoons butter (but do not brown)
small stalk celery, chopped	
mixed herbs	
a few peppercorns	sauce: in a saucepan melt 3 tablespoons butter, stir in the flour (but do not brown), and gradually add the veal stock, stirring
8 mushrooms	
12 small white onions	
2 tablespoons butter	add the egg thickening (made by mixing the egg yolks and lemon juice). pour in the cream, add the veal, and simmer a few minutes without boiling
3 tablespoons butter	
¼ cup flour	
¾ pint veal stock	to serve, place the veal in a warm serving dish, pour over the sauce, and garnish with the mushrooms and onions. sprinkle with chopped parsley
the yolks of 2 eggs	
the juice of 1 lemon	
6 tablespoons cream	
1 teaspoon chopped parsley	

40

BOEUF À LA BOURGUIGNONNE
(*Beef, Burgundy Style*)

Start with cubes of beef, salt pork, onions, and Burgundy wine and no matter what you do you'll end up with Boeuf Bourguignonne.

2 ounces salt pork, cubed (or use 6 slices bacon)

put salt pork or bacon in a heavy skillet and cook until all the fat has run out. remove the pork and save

2 pounds beef (chuck or rump), cut into 2-inch cubes

flour, if you wish

brown the beef cubes (flour them first, if you wish) in the pork fat along with the onions and garlic

2 onions, sliced

1 clove garlic, crushed

salt and pepper (freshly ground is best)

season with salt and pepper, add shallots, thyme, and bay leaf and pour in ½ bottle wine. cover and simmer slowly for 3 hours or until beef is tender

2 shallots or 1 leek, chopped

½ bay leaf

add mushrooms, if you wish, and cook 5 minutes longer

½ teaspoon thyme

½ bottle red Burgundy

just before serving, flambé a little cognac and add to the stew

½ pound button (or sliced) mushrooms, if you wish

(serves 4)

2 or 3 ounces cognac

41

COEUR À LA CRÈME *(Cream Cheese Hearts)*

This is an elegant dessert and easy to make. But it should be made in little heart-shaped molds or baskets, and who has heart-shaped molds lying around? Anyway here's how to make it and if you don't feel like finding the molds, invent something.

1 pound cottage cheese	strain the cheese through a sieve and add the sugar and vanilla
2 tablespoons confectioners' sugar	
½ teaspoon vanilla	whip the cream and mix with the cheese until smooth and well blended
1 cup iced heavy cream	
whites of 3 eggs	beat the egg whites and add to the mixture, blending well
crushed strawberries, fresh or frozen	spoon the mixture into individual heart-shaped baskets or molds and place in refrigerator overnight to drain
	serve in or out of the molds on chilled plates. top each *coeur* with a bit of crushed strawberries
	(serves **6**)

42

CRÊPES SUZETTE

Every chef has his own particular method of making *Crêpes Suzette*. Here is one of the better-known methods. Before you show off before the guests, better try it out by yourself.

4 lumps sugar	rub the sugar lumps over the orange until all sides have absorbed the aromatic oil. squeeze the orange and save the juice
1 orange	
½ cup butter	
2 ounces maraschino	crush the sugar lumps, and cream with half the butter
2 ounces curaçao	
2 ounces kirsch, warmed	put the rest of the butter into a skillet or chafing dish, melt and add the orange-butter, orange juice, maraschino, and curaçao, and blend well with a wooden spoon
	add the kirsch and ignite
	put in the *crêpes* one at a time, turn and fold into quarters. spoon on the juices and serve at once
	(serves 4)

43

CRÊPES (*French Pancakes*)

The glamorous *crêpes* are nothing more than French pancakes. They can be served rolled around creamed chicken or seafood. Sweeten them (as in the following recipe), spread with pineapple or jelly, top with ice cream, raisins, almonds, or whatever you have around, and/or flambé with brandy or kirsch.

2 eggs	put all but the last two ingredients into an electric blender. turn it on, turn it off. then you have the perfect batter (for 12 *crêpes*) in an instant
1 cup milk	
¾ cup flour	
1 teaspoon oil	
pinch salt	to cook, heat a 6-inch frying pan, grease lightly with a little oil and a little butter, and pour in 2 tablespoons batter for each *crêpe*, cook until lightly browned on both sides. *Voilà*
1½ teaspoons sugar	
1½ teaspoons kirsch	
a little oil	
a little butter	

PÊCHES MELBA (*Peaches Melba*)

1 package frozen raspberries	thaw the raspberries and mash, add the jelly, and simmer over low heat for a few minutes, then add the cornstarch mixed with the water and simmer, stirring, until clear. put aside until cool
4 tablespoons currant, raspberry, or some other kind of jelly	
1 teaspoon cornstarch	
1 tablespoon water	place the peach halves, hollow side up, in dessert dishes, top with ice cream, and pour over the sauce
6 peach halves (canned)	
vanilla ice cream	
	(serves 6)

44

3

WHO
NEEDS
AN
IRISH
COOKBOOK

WHO NEEDS AN IRISH COOKBOOK

PRAWNS, DUBLIN BAY STYLE

IRISH PÂTÉ

IRISH POTATO SOUP

MUTTON BROTH

IRISH STEW

IRISH HAM

CORNED BEEF AND CABBAGE

TRIPE AND ONIONS

IRISH WHISKEY CAKE

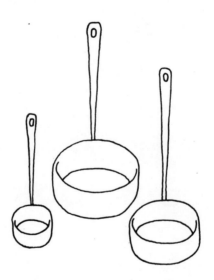

The Irish don't go overboard for cocktail snacks or appetizers. When they want to eat there's no horsing around with hors d'oeuvres. They sit down at the table and start right in on good solid food.

But for Americans who like an appetizer before dinner or with a drink there are lots of Irish delicacies to choose from.

Every fall there's salmon roe, juicy and red and much larger than sturgeon roe or caviar. There are kippers—herrings salted and smoked, filleted and broiled.

And there are Dublin Bay prawns, sweet, tender, and ocean-tasting. Here is a good way to fix them:

PRAWNS, DUBLIN BAY STYLE

live (if you can get them) prawns or shrimp or scampi	throw the prawns into the boiling water and cook until pink. remove and cool
boiling water (this shouldn't give you much trouble)	remove from the shell and serve on lettuce topped with mayonnaise and capers
lettuce	
mayonnaise	
capers	

47

IRISH PÂTÉ

½ pound chicken livers or pork livers, or even calves liver	cut the livers into pieces and remove veins
¼ cup chicken stock	place in a saucepan with the stock, whiskey, and seasonings, and marinate a couple of hours, stirring occasionally. then simmer gently for 15 or 20 minutes
jigger Irish whiskey	
a bay leaf	
pinch thyme	cool, remove bay leaf, and put into a blender. add the butter little by little and blend until everything is well mixed
salt and pepper	
pinch cayenne	
pinch powdered cloves	spoon into a dish, chill, and slice. serve on crackers
pinch powdered mace	
¼ pound butter	

The Irish are fine warm people but their weather during the greater part of the year is bitter cold. Except in the cities, heating systems in the homes are rare and the hearty Irish have come to rely pretty much on a personal internal heating system. Well, you can't drink whiskey all the time and so between drinks you eat soup.

In Ireland, perhaps more than anywhere else, soup is a casual dish, prepared casually and with an ever changing taste. This is because most of the good family soups are made by tossing

48

whatever you have on hand—leftovers and warmed-overs—into the pot.

Of course, since potatoes are the national staple, they are often the basis for whatever soup finally evolves. So let's start from the beginning with:

IRISH POTATO SOUP

1 cup butter

in a heavy pan melt the butter. add the potatoes and onions, toss well, cover and cook very slowly for about 15 minutes, but do not brown

4 onions, thinly sliced

8 potatoes, peeled and thinly sliced

2 quarts milk

add the milk and all the other ingredients (except the chives) and simmer for half an hour

2 cloves garlic, crushed

a couple of pinches each of mace and thyme, a bay leaf and some parsley

throw out the parsley and bay leaf and put through a soup strainer. serve hot, garnished with chopped chives

salt and pepper

pinch of cayenne

chopped chives

this recipe will make enough for a couple of days (like a dozen servings) so tomorrow you can throw in your leftovers (chicken, turkey, duck, lamb, or veal) and you'll have a new soup

49

(serves 4)

MUTTON BROTH

2 pounds stewing mutton or lamb, cut into pieces — boil the mutton in 2 quarts water for 10 minutes and remove the scum

5 tablespoons pearl barley

salt and pepper

Worcestershire sauce — add the barley, salt and pepper and Worcestershire, cover and simmer for an hour and a half

about a cup chopped carrot

about a cup chopped turnip

chopped leek or onion (or both) — add the remaining ingredients, cover and simmer an hour longer, adding more water if needed. remove the meat bone, chop the meat, and serve

chopped parsley — this will heat up 8 or 10 winter diners

about a cup chopped celery

couple cloves garlic, chopped

50

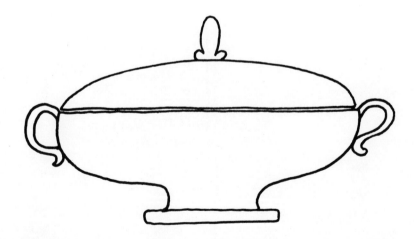

IRISH STEW

You can make a stew just about any way you want (and the Irish do). But there are certain differences, sometimes very small, that distinguish one stew from another. Goulash is different from Bourguignonne, Brunswick is different from chicken stew, and Irish stew differs from lamb stew.

A woman I know served up a delicious Irish stew for some Irish friends of hers. In it she put lamb, onions, garlic, flour, mushrooms, milk, and some seasonings. Question: What did she do wrong? Answer: She gave it the wrong name. Authentic Irish stew needs no flour; it gets its thickening from potatoes.

The original Irish stew was made from kid (the meat was left over after the skin went into glove-making). Today you use mutton or lamb, but you never, never use goat.

3 pounds stewing lamb, mutton (or kid, if you can get it)

remove the fat from the meat and cut into pieces. use the bone to get extra flavor

a dozen medium potatoes, peeled

slice half the potatoes thinly, leaving the rest whole

4 or 5 onions, sliced

pinch thyme

salt and pepper

put everything except the whole potatoes into a large pot, season well, add a couple of cups of water, cover and simmer 1½ hours. toss in the whole potatoes, cover and simmer another hour or until potatoes are done. you will have enough stew to feed 6

the thinly sliced potatoes dissolve and thicken the stew while the whole potatoes retain their shape. you can add carrots and turnips (or almost anything else) to the stew but most Irish regard such practices as vulgar

(serves about 6)

51

IRISH HAM

Irish hams are different. They're dry soft-cured and then boned before they are smoked. (And they are often peat-smoked.) The skin and most of the waste fat is trimmed off and the entire meat is neatly squared up.

ham	soak the ham overnight to desalt and soften
2 quarts Irish stout (or use American beer and a teaspoon of blackstrap molasses)	put it in a large pot with the stout and sugar, and add enough cold water to cover
about ½ cup sugar	bring to a boil and simmer to a slow bubble for about a half hour per pound or until tender to a fork-test. the trick is to cook it slowly
	let it cool in the cooking beer and remove the skin (if any). slice thin
	if you like your ham baked, cover it with breadcrumbs, mustard, and brown sugar mixed to a goo with a little of the cooking beer. stud with cloves and shove into a preheated 400° oven for a few minutes to brown

CORNED BEEF AND CABBAGE

corned beef (the best cuts are from the brisket or ribs)	wash the brine from the beef, tie it up, put it into a large pot, cover with cold water, and boil for 5 minutes
thyme	
parsley	remove the scum, add some thyme, parsley, onion, carrot, and pepper (it doesn't really matter how much of these you use—you can't go wrong)
onion	
carrot	
pepper	simmer about 3 hours. remove the scum again, add the
cabbage, cut into quarters	cabbage, cover and simmer for about a half hour longer or until the cabbage is cooked
	cabbage can be cooked in separate water to which has been added some of the corned beef water. this is a good idea when the corned beef is too salty

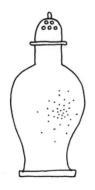 

53

TRIPE AND ONIONS

Tripe is the stomach lining of sheep. It comes three ways: honey-comb (the best), smooth, and pocket. And you can get it fresh, pickled, or canned. It's good—if you like it—and very digestible.

2 pounds tripe	wash the tripe and bring to a quick boil in salted water.
3 cups milk	remove from the heat, wash again, and cut into 2-inch
3 onions, chopped	squares
1 bay leaf	put the tripe, milk, onions, bay leaf, and salt and pepper into
salt and pepper	a saucepan, cover and simmer for an hour or so, or until
2 tablespoons butter	tripe is tender
2 tablespoons flour	in a skillet melt the butter, add the flour, cook for a minute,
3 slices bacon, cooked and crumbled	then add some of the milk from the tripe and make a smooth sauce
	strain off the liquid from the tripe and onions, add the bacon and the sauce
	(serves 4–6)

54

IRISH WHISKEY CAKE

the rind of a lemon

a jigger of Irish whiskey

1 cup dried raisins

½ pound butter

½ cup sugar

3 eggs

2 cups cake flour

pinch salt

½ teaspoon baking powder

soak the lemon peel and raisins in the whiskey for an hour or so—then throw away the lemon peel

cream the butter and sugar. beat in the eggs one at a time

sift the flour, salt, and baking powder together and fold into the egg mixture

fold in the whiskey-raisin mixture, put into a well oiled and floured 7-inch cake pan, and bake at 350° for 1½ hours

55

4

WHO
NEEDS
A
MEXICAN
COOKBOOK

WHO NEEDS A MEXICAN COOKBOOK

GUACAMOLE

CHILI CON QUESO (*Chili with Cheese*)

SOPA DE ALMEJAS À LA MEXICANA
(*Mexican Clam Soup*)

SOPA DE GARBANZOS (*Garbanzo Soup*)

HUEVOS RANCHEROS (*Eggs, Ranch Style*)

ARROZ CON POLLO (*Rice with Chicken*)

BIFTEC À LA MEXICANA (*Steak, Mexican Style*)

CHILI CON CARNE (*Chili with Beef*)

TACOS DE CARNE MOLICA (*Chopped Beef Tacos*)

CAPIROTADA (*Mexican Bread Pudding*)

FLAN

MEXICAN BEVERAGES

Mexican dishes are mostly a blending of several ingredients: meat and/or fish and/or beans and/or cornmeal and/or rice deliciously flavored with condiments and spices not commonly used in American cooking.

You don't need a cookbook to make most of these wonderful dishes, but you will need a few special supplies or your dish won't have the delectable flavor of old Mexico.

You'll need chiles (peppers to you). They come in all colors—green, brown, red, yellow; in all sizes; and in all flavors from mild and sweet (pimientos) to fiery hot (the tiny piquin or tepin). They come fresh, canned, dried, and powdered.

You'll need beans. There are many kinds, but you can settle for Mexican dried pink beans or canned kidney beans for most dishes.

You'll need a few spices such as cumin (comino) seed or powder, oregano (wild marjoram), coriander, and maybe anise, but you probably have most of these already.

And you'll need masa, a moist, ground corn preparation, used for making tortillas. You can get fresh masa or packaged tortilla flour which needs only to be mixed with water. Or you can get ready-made tortillas in a can.

All the above can be found almost anywhere in Texas and California or, if that's too far away from your house, there are Mexican supply stores in most large cities throughout the country.

And finally you'll need to know the names of some of the very common everyday foods indigenous only to Mexico, such as:

tortillas—thin cakes made of masa flour (a moist, fresh-ground Mexican corn preparation).

tacos—Mexican sandwiches: rolled or folded tortillas stuffed with various fillings. They may be grilled, fried, baked, or just warmed, served plain or with a sauce.

enchiladas—tortillas dipped in sauce, spread with a filling, rolled, and fried.

tostadas—tortillas that have been fried in oil until golden brown and crisp.

tamales—corn husks spread with masa flour and wrapped around a filling.

59

GUACAMOLE

Here is a good Mexican dip, well known in the United States. Anybody can make it without a cookbook by just mashing together avocados and tomatoes with a few condiments. I have spelled out this particular recipe but you can do almost anything you like without messing it up. Try adding chopped peanuts or bits of crisp bacon or coriander.

2 very ripe avocados	cut the avocados in half, peel, and remove seeds. put avocados and all the other ingredients into a blender
2 tomatoes, peeled	
1 onion, finely chopped	
1 clove garlic, crushed	chill in the refrigerator and serve as a dip with fried tortillas (tostadas, to you), as a spread with mayonnaise, or as a salad with lettuce and tomatoes
2 tablespoons lemon juice or vinegar	
3 tablespoons chopped green chiles	
salt to taste	guacamole turns brown when exposed to the air, so arrange to keep it in a tightly closed container until ready for use

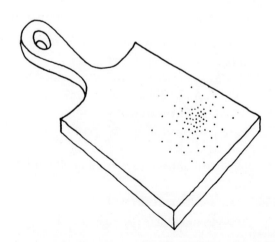

CHILI CON QUESO *(Chili with Cheese)*

1 onion, minced

2 tablespoons butter

1 tomato, peeled and chopped

½ can green chiles, peeled and chopped

salt and pepper

½ teaspoon chili powder

½ pound Monterey Jack (or cream cheese), cut into bits

1 cup sour cream (or sweet cream)

melt the butter and add onion, tomato, chiles, salt and pepper, and chili powder, stir well

add the cheese and, when it is melted, the cream

serve as a cocktail dip with tostaditos, on toast or crackers

SOPA DE ALMEJAS À LA MEXICANA
(Mexican Clam Soup)

2 dozen cherrystone clams

1 onion, chopped

1 clove garlic, crushed

3 tablespoons olive oil

½ cup tomato sauce

chopped parsley

½ teaspoon chili powder

salt and pepper

scrub clams well, put them in a pot, add 2 cups of water and some salt, and cook until shells open

throw out the shells, chop the clams coarsely, add them and all the other ingredients to the broth, and simmer a little, adding more water if needed

(serves 4)

61

SOPA DE GARBANZOS *(Mexican Garbanzo Soup)*

½ pound dried garbanzo beans (chick-peas)	soak the beans overnight
a ham bone	drain, add a couple of quarts of fresh water, the bone, and some salt. cover and simmer
salt	an hour
¼ pound salt pork, cubed	fry the pork and onions with the chili powder and add to
2 onions, chopped	the beans. cover again and simmer a half hour longer
1 teaspoon chili powder	
2 potatoes, peeled and cubed	add the potatoes and sausage and cook a few minutes until the potatoes are done
½ pound longaniza sausage, Italian sausage, hot dogs, or salami, cut into pieces	(serves 6)

HUEVOS RANCHEROS *(Eggs, Ranch Style)*

62

2 tablespoons bacon fat or oil	heat the bacon fat in a small saucepan, add the onion and
1 tablespoon minced onion	garlic, and simmer gently
½ clove garlic, crushed	add the oregano, tomato sauce, chiles, and salt,
couple pinches oregano	continuing to simmer
½ cup tomato sauce	fry the eggs, one by one, in the sauce and serve with the
1 or 2 green chiles, peeled and washed and chopped (or a teaspoon chili powder)	sauce poured over them
salt	(serves 2)
4 eggs	

ARROZ CON POLLO (*Rice with Chicken*)

Here's a chicken that can be found in every Mexican pot—in every pot in Spain, too, since that's where it came from. A chicken stew, almost anything you have can go into it, but it's *got* to have saffron.

½ cup olive oil	using a large, heavy skillet, sauté the onions and garlic in the oil. salt the chicken pieces, add them to the skillet and brown on all sides
1 clove garlic, minced	
1 onion, chopped	
1 frying chicken, cut into serving pieces	put in the tomato sauce, saffron, pepper, and broth. cover and cook about 20 minutes
1 teaspoon salt	
¼ cup tomato sauce	put in the rice, stir, cover again and cook one half hour longer or until all the liquid has been absorbed and the chicken is tender
pinch of powdered saffron	
pepper	
3 cups chicken broth	if you want to add a bay leaf, a little oregano, some chopped pimientos, peas, or anything else, who's stopping you
1 cup uncooked rice	

(serves 4)

63

BIFTEC À LA MEXICANA (*Steak, Mexican Style*)

½ cup olive oil (*or some other kind*)

1 clove garlic, crushed

1 onion, chopped

½ green pepper, chopped

½ cup flour

1 teaspoon salt

pepper

½ teaspoon chili powder

1½ pounds round steak (½ inch thick)

1 cup tomato sauce

½ cup stuffed olives

using a heavy skillet, sauté the garlic, onions, and green pepper gently in the oil for a few minutes, remove, and set aside

meanwhile, mix the flour, salt, pepper, and chili powder, and pound it into both sides of the steak (you can use the edge of a plate)

place the steak into the hot skillet and brown quickly on both sides

reduce the heat and add the sautéed vegetables and tomato sauce, cover and cook until meat is tender (like 1½ hours)

thin the sauce with a little water, beer, or red wine, add stuffed olives, and serve

(serves 4)

CHILI CON CARNE (*Chili with Beef*)

You want to cook up a batch of chili. First thing you do is look it up in a cookbook? Wrong! First thing you do is to get hold of some meat, some chiles, some onions, and a little oregano and cumin. Then let your conscience be your guide.

If your conscience needs guiding start with this recipe for a delicious soupy chili from Mexico.

3 tablespoons olive oil

2 cloves garlic, crushed

1 large onion, chopped

2 pounds beef, cubed or chopped (if you haven't got beef, use lean pork)

10 dried chiles (if you can't find them use a couple tablespoons chili powder)

1 teaspoon oregano

1 teaspoon cumin seed, crushed

1 teaspoon salt

2 cups beef bouillon

in a large heavy skillet sauté the garlic and onions in olive oil for a couple of minutes, throw in the meat, and brown

remove the stems, seeds, and skins from the chiles (boiling them for about 15 minutes will make this easier)

add the chili, oregano, ground cumin seed, and salt to the meat. pour in the bouillon and cook until the meat is tender and the flavors are well blended

you serve this chili in a bowl with Mexican pink beans (that have been soaked overnight and boiled until tender) or canned kidney beans diluted with a little water. control the heat by using more (or less) of the liquid from the bean pot

vary the dish by adding a cup canned tomatoes and/or a minced green pepper. you can put in a little celery seed, cayenne, bay leaf, basil, or almost anything your heartburn desires

65

it is hard to cook chili too long. it is even better reheated the next day

(serves 6–8)

TACOS DE CARNE MOLICA *(Chopped Beef Tacos)*

6 tablespoons oil

1 onion, chopped

1 pound lean ground beef

1 green pepper, chopped

1 clove garlic, crushed

1 cup tomatoes

½ teaspoon chili powder

½ teaspoon oregano

salt

12 tortillas

cook the meat and onion in 2 tablespoons of the oil until brown, using a heavy skillet

add the remaining ingredients and cook 20 minutes longer

warm the tortillas, spread them with the meat mixture, roll, and turn upside down

fry them in the remaining oil until crisp

(serves 6)

66

CAPIROTADA *(Mexican Bread Pudding)*

1 pound brown sugar

stick cinnamon

1 clove

1 tablespoon butter

6 slices toast, cut into cubes

3 cups sliced apples and/or peaches, bananas, berries, etc.

1 cup raisins

1 cup chopped nuts (any kind)

½ pound cheese, cut into bits (Monterey Jack, cream cheese, or mozzarella)

put the sugar, cinnamon, and clove into a quart of water and boil down to a syrup. discard cinnamon and clove

take a casserole and butter it well. put in a layer of toast, cover with a layer of the fruit, sprinkle with raisins and nuts, and lay on bits of cheese

repeat the layers until all the ingredients have been used

pour the syrup over the pudding and bake at 325° for one half hour

(serves 4–6)

67

FLAN

This is only a caramel custard, but it's very popular in Mexico—and it's good!

1½ cups sugar	put 1 cup of sugar into an 8-inch cake pan and place over low heat. stir constantly until sugar melts and carmelizes. tilt the pan until entire surface is coated. then let it cool
8 eggs	
1 can evaporated milk	
½ cup cream	
2 teaspoons vanilla	in a bowl beat the eggs, add the milk, cream, remaining sugar, and vanilla. pour this custard into the cake pan, cover and place pan in a larger pan containing about ½ inch of hot water
2 jiggers rum (or brandy)	
	bake in a 325° oven for 45 minutes or until set
	cool for several hours, turn out onto a platter, douse with warm rum, and ignite
	(serves about 8)

68

try adding a couple tablespoons of cocoa, or ¼ pound of blanched ground almonds or other nuts, or 1 cup grated coconut to the above recipe—or think up a variation of your own
there are all kinds of flan: orange flan, coconut flan, banana flan, pineapple flan, chocolate, coffee, or orange

MEXICAN BEVERAGES

Mexicans drink *café con leche* (coffee with milk) and Mexican chocolate made by dissolving a square of sweetened chocolate in hot milk and beating with a wooden twirler until foamy. They also drink cocktails made mostly on a tequila base, the most famous of which is a Margarita (3 parts tequila, 1 part Cointreau, and ½ lime, iced and served in a stem glass with a salt-coated rim), tequila neat (you put a little salt on the back of your hand, lick it, toss off the shot of tequila, and suck a lemon), and mescal, the poor man's tequila.

Then there is *aguardiente,* a brandy, and *pulque* (fermented cactus juice). *Sangria* (lemon, orange, and sugar mixed with red wine, served iced in a tall glass) is a favorite hot-weather drink borrowed from Spain.

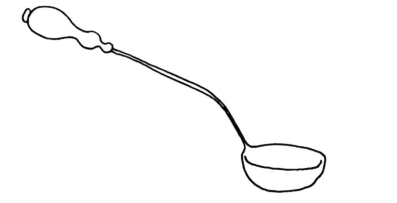

69

5

WHO
NEEDS
AN
ITALIAN
COOKBOOK

STRACCIATELLA (*Roman Consommé*)

ACQUA COTTA(*Cooked Water*)

MINESTRONE (*Vegetable Soup*)

PASTA

SPAGHETTI AL OLIO ED AGLIO
(*Spaghetti with Oil and Garlic*)

SPAGHETTI ALLA NAPOLITANA
(*Spaghetti, Neapolitan Style*)

SPAGHETTI CON SALSA DI VONGOLE
(*Spaghetti with Clam Sauce*)

FETTUCCINE ALLA ROMANA (*Fettucini with Anchovies*)

TAGLIATELLE AL PROSCIUTTO ALLA BOLOGNESE
(*Tagliatelle with Ham*)

ZUPPA DI CROSTACEI (*Shellfish Soup*)

ZUPPA DI VONGOLE (*Clam Soup*)

ARAGOSTA FRA DIAVOLO (*Lobster Fra Diablo*)

CONCHIGLI AL FERRI (*Broiled Scallops*)

POLLO ALLA CACCIATORA (*Chicken Cacciatora*)

POLLO ALLA ROMANA (*Chicken, Roman Style*)

PICCIONCINI ARROSTI (*Roast Squab*)

POLPETTE (*Meat Balls*)

SCALOPPINE DI VITELLO (*Veal Cutlets*)

SCALOPPINE MILANESE (*Cutlets, Milanese Style*)

COSTOLETTE BOLOGNESE(*Cutlets, Bolognese Style*)

SCALOPPINE AL MARSALA (*Cutlets Marsala*)

SALTIMBOCCA ALLA ROMANA (*Cutlets, Roman Style*)

OSSO BUCO MILANESE (*Veal Shin, Milanese Style*)

ZUPPA INGLESE (*English Cake*)

PESCHE AL VINO (*Peaches in Wine*)

You always thought of the French as the greatest cooks in all of Europe? Well, the Italians made them what they are today.

Back in the sixteenth century you couldn't touch Venice for the splendor of its banquets and feasts and for the infinite variety and delicacy of the food which adorned its tables. So that in 1533 when Catherine de' Medici went to take up residence in France, she took along with her a team of famous Italian chefs. France has never been the same since.

Meanwhile, back in Italy—a country of independent city-states, geographical and climatic extremes, diversified customs and dialects—the widest possible variety of regional dishes emerged.

Pasta they all eat, and fine wines and seafood abound everywhere, but by and large there is only slight relationship between the cookery of the cool, mountainous regions of the North and hot, flat southern country.

A gentleman from the North country one day found himself in Naples (or so an old story goes), went to one of the leading restaurants there, and ordered dinner. He had gone through the numerous courses and came to the end of the meal when the waiter asked him whether he might like some ice cream for dessert. "Yes," he replied, "but please without the tomato sauce."

This book gives you a sampling of the foods from all the regions of the country: dishes from Piedmont, Milan, Genoa, Venice, from Bologna and Florence, from Rome, and from Naples and the South.

STRACCIATELLA (*Roman Consommé*)   **73**

6 cups chicken broth	heat the chicken broth, but do not boil
3 eggs, beaten	gradually stir in the beaten eggs, the minced parsley, and the cheese
2 tablespoons finely minced parsley	
2 tablespoons grated Romano cheese (no Parmesan)	serve at once (enough for 6)

ACQUA COTTA (*Cooked Water*)

This clear soup of southern Italy is made of water, rather than stock. It must contain eggs, should have mushrooms, and has to be served with Italian bread fried in butter or oil. Otherwise you can make it from almost any ingredients you happen to have around.

1 pound sliced mushroom caps	sauté the mushrooms and garlic in the oil for 5 minutes and remove the garlic
1 clove garlic	
½ cup olive oil	add the vegetables. cook gently for 15 minutes longer, then add the water. season, cover and simmer for an hour
vegetables such as chopped tomatoes, celery, onion, pepper, chopped carrot, etc.	
4 cups water	stir in gradually the egg-cheese mixture and serve at once with the croutons
salt and pepper	(serves 4)
3 eggs, beaten with 3 tablespoons grated Parmesan cheese	
sliced Italian bread fried in oil or butter	

MINESTRONE *(Vegetable Soup)*

Minestrone is found all over Italy. The ingredients vary somewhat from region to region and so does the emphasis on such things as oil, tomatoes, garlic, and pasta. Sometimes even rice is added. So in making minestrone let your conscience (and the contents of your pantry) be your guide—or be guided by the following recipe from central Italy.

1 cup some kind of dried beans that have soaked overnight

simmer the beans in the water (with salt) for about an hour, using a large pot

3 quarts water

couple teaspoons salt

throw in the vegetables and cook another hour

vegetables such as cut-up cabbage, diced carrots, diced turnips

meanwhile, in a skillet sauté the onion, garlic, and salt pork in butter and oil. when the onion is soft add the tomato and parsley and cook slowly for about 20 minutes

1 onion, sliced

1 clove garlic, crushed

a half hour before the soup is done add the sautéed mixture and a cup of pasta. serve with grated Parmesan cheese

¼ pound salt pork, diced

tablespoon butter

tablespoon olive oil

(serves 8)

1 tomato, peeled and chopped

75

1 tablespoon chopped parsley

1 cup some kind of pasta, broken into bits

grated Parmesan cheese

PASTA

In Italy there are more shapes, sizes, and varieties of pasta than anywhere else in the world—except perhaps China. Pasta comes thick and thin, round and flat, wide and narrow, solid and hollow, straight, twisted, angled, tied in knots, and stuffed. And each variety has its own name: spaghetti, vermicelli, tagliatelle, fettucini, lasagne, ravioli . . .

Pasta is eaten almost anytime—for lunch as a complete meal or for dinner as an entrée—and it is blended with an almost unbelievable variety of sauces.

Anybody can cook pasta, but you've got to follow the Italian rules strictly to cook it right. Here are the rules for spaghetti.

Uno. You don't break it or chop it or otherwise disfigure it. If it comes a yard long, stand it on end in a pot of boiling water and it will gradually collapse and sink into the pot on its own.

Due. Don't spare the water—use lots (at least 6 quarts per pound of spaghetti) and salt it well. (Skimp on water and you'll get sodden spaghetti.)

Tre. Don't overboil. Spaghetti should be cooked "al dente"— done, but firm to the tooth. Six to eight minutes should be about right, but chew on a strand as you cook it and you'll know when to stop.

Quattro. Add a tablespoon of oil to the pot for the last two minutes of cooking to keep the spaghetti from sticking together when it is drained.

Cinque. Drain it well in a colander or wrap it in a hot napkin as the Neapolitans do. Wet spaghetti is unpardonable.

76

Sei. Serve it hot. Before the spaghetti is done, you should already have prepared the sauce.

SPAGHETTI AL OLIO ED AGLIO
(*Spaghetti with Oil and Garlic*)

½ cup olive oil	in a small saucepan heat the oil but do not boil
2–4 cloves garlic, chopped	turn off the heat, add the garlic, and let stand a minute or so
½ cup minced parsley	add the parsley and stir the sauce into the spaghetti
	serve with grated Parmesan cheese if you wish, but in Genoa the cheese is usually left off
	(if you have used a pound of spaghetti, this will serve 4–6)

SPAGHETTI ALLA NAPOLITANA
(*Spaghetti, Neapolitan Style*)

3 tablespoons olive oil	in a small saucepan heat the oil, garlic, and onion (do not burn)
2 cloves garlic, chopped	
1 onion, chopped	add the ham and sausage and cook for about 4 minutes
3 tablespoons ham, chopped	
½ pound Italian sausage, chopped	pour in the bouillon and tomato sauce, cover and simmer slowly for 10 or 15 minutes
½ cup canned bouillon	
1 cup canned tomato sauce	stir the sauce into the spaghetti and sprinkle with grated Parmesan cheese
grated Parmesan cheese	(if you have used a pound of spaghetti, this will serve 4–6)

77

SPAGHETTI CON SALSA DI VONGOLE
(*Spaghetti with Clam Sauce*)

You can make this a lot of ways (with tomatoes it's red clam sauce; without, it's white).

½ cup olive oil

in a small saucepan heat the oil and garlic (do not burn)

2 cloves garlic, chopped

pinch dried marjoram, thyme, basil, and/or oregano

add all the ingredients except the clams and parsley and cook about an hour. add the clams and parsley and cook 5 minutes longer

1 cup canned or fresh tomatoes and 1 can tomato paste (if you wish)

2 cups clam juice (strained)

stir the sauce into the spaghetti and serve without cheese

a little pepper

(if you have used a pound of spaghetti, this will serve 4–6)

2 cups chopped clams

2 tablespoons chopped parsley

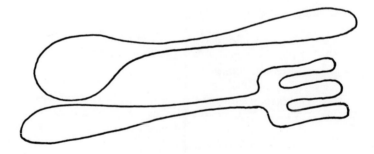

FETTUCCINE ALLA ROMANA
(Fettucini with Anchovies)

6 quarts salted water	cook the noodles "al dente" in the boiling water
1 pound narrow egg noodles	
7 tablespoons sweet butter	meanwhile, mash the anchovy fillets and cream them into the butter
6 anchovy fillets	drain the fettucini, mix well with the anchovy-butter, and serve immediately
	(serves **6**)

TAGLIATELLE AL PROSCIUTTO ALLA BOLOGNESE *(Tagliatelle with Ham)*

6 quarts salted water	cook the noodles "al dente" in the boiling water
1 pound narrow egg noodles	
7 tablespoons sweet butter	meanwhile, melt the butter (do not brown) and add the ham
1 cup ham (or prosciutto), finely diced	drain the tagliatelle, mix well with the butter-ham and cheese. serve at once
½ cup grated Parmesan cheese	(serves **6**)

79

ZUPPA DI CROSTACEI (*Shellfish Soup*)

The Italians call all kinds of things *zuppa* (even a dessert). Some soup! This one is a meal.

½ cup olive oil	in a large casserole gently simmer the onions, garlic, parsley, and tomato in the oil for 5 or 6 minutes
2 chopped onions	
4 cloves garlic, minced	
1 tablespoon chopped parsley	add the wine and simmer 5 minutes longer
2 cups chopped tomato	put in the shellfish, 2 cups boiling water, a bay leaf, a pinch saffron, salt and pepper. cook briskly for 15 minutes
1 cup dry white wine	
3 dozen small clams, scrubbed	
1½ pounds lobster, cut into 6 pieces	add a tablespoon butter, swish the mixture around, and pour the broth into 6 hot soup plates with fried slices of bread
the legs and cracked claws of 6 crabs	
2 cups boiling water	serve the shellfish on top
a bay leaf	(serves 6)
pinch saffron	
salt and pepper	
1 tablespoon butter	
6 slices Italian bread, fried in butter	

80

ZUPPA DI VONGOLE (*Clam Soup*)

This is a simpler version of the above. Make with clams, olive oil, tomato juice, minced parsley, a little oregano, and a dash of cayenne. Serve it on fried Italian bread.

ARAGOSTA FRA DIAVOLO (*Lobster Fra Diablo*)

¼ *cup olive oil*	simmer the garlic gently in the oil using a small saucepan
2 cloves garlic, crushed	add the tomato, wine, parsley, oregano, and pepper and cook slowly for about 20 minutes
2 cups tomato puree	
½ *cup dry red wine*	place the lobsters in a large baking dish, split side up, spoon the sauce over them, and bake about 8 minutes in a preheated oven
1 tablespoon chopped parsley	
1 teaspoon oregano	
dash cayenne pepper	(serves 4)
4 1½-pound lobsters, boiled, split, and claw-cracked	

CONCHIGLI AL FERRI (*Broiled Scallops*)

1 pound scallops	thread the scallops and bacon slices alternately on skewers and broil under a hot flame, turning to cook all sides
8 slices bacon, cut into quarters	
2 tablespoons olive oil	meanwhile, in a small saucepan very gently heat the oil and butter with the remaining ingredients without browning
2 tablespoons butter	
1 clove garlic, crushed	
1 scallion, minced	pour the sauce over the skewered scallops
1 tablespoon chopped parsley	
salt and pepper	(serves 4)

81

POLLO ALLA CACCIATORA *(Chicken Cacciatora)*

1 4-pound chicken, cut into serving pieces

in a large heavy skillet brown the chicken pieces on all sides in the oil-butter mixture and remove

2 tablespoons olive oil

2 tablespoons butter

1 large onion, sliced

to the same skillet add the onion, garlic, salt and pepper, basil, and parsley. simmer slowly about 3 minutes

1 clove garlic, crushed

salt and pepper

add the tomato paste, wine, and chicken pieces, cover and cook about one half hour or until the chicken is tender

pinch dried basil

teaspoon chopped parsley

(serves 4)

1 can tomato paste

1 cup red wine

82

POLLO ALLA ROMANA *(Chicken, Roman Style)*

Do as the Romans do. Leave out the basil and onion, add a little rosemary and a couple slices of ham or prosciutto cut into pieces and you have an entirely different dish.

You can produce other entirely different dishes, too. Try adding ripe olives (or green), salt pork, Parmesan cheese. Try it without the tomato paste.

PICCIONCINI ARROSTI (*Roast Squab*)

In Milan they eat a lot of squab. The square in front of the great Milan Cathedral is thick with pigeons. Is this a coincidence? Anyway, you catch a squab (from your butcher), wash it and dry it and rub it all over, inside and out, with salt and pepper and rosemary. You tie strips of bacon across the breast, truss it, and roast it about a half hour, or until brown and tender. If you have a friend, you'll need another bird.

POLPETTE (*Meat Balls*)

1 pound lean ground beef

2 teaspoons minced parsley

1 clove garlic, crushed

1 strip lemon peel, grated

salt and pepper

nutmeg

3 tablespoons dry breadcrumbs

1 egg, beaten

olive oil

mix all ingredients together and form into 8 cakes or balls

cook slowly in oil for 3 or 4 minutes and serve with spaghetti

(serves 4)

83

SCALOPPINE DI VITELLO (*Veal Cutlets*)

The favorite meat of all Italy is veal, and most often it is served as a cutlet, sliced very thin and pounded still thinner into ½-inch-thick slabs about 5 inches long. But no two regions of the country agree what should be done from then on. Here's the way they do it in Milan.

SCALOPPINE MILANESE *(Cutlets, Milanese Style)*

8 cutlets	soak the cutlets in milk for about an hour. drain and dry
a little milk	
salt and pepper	season with salt and pepper and dip first in flour, then in egg, and then in breadcrumbs
½ cup flour	
2 eggs, beaten	melt the butter and oil in a heavy skillet, put in the cutlets, turn almost at once, and sauté over low heat for about 5 minutes. turn again and cook 5 minutes longer until they are golden crisp
1 cup breadcrumbs	
½ cup olive oil	
½ cup butter	
4 lemon slices	place on a heated platter, pour on the pan juices, and serve with lemon slices and parsley
minced parsley	
	(serves 4)

COSTOLETTE BOLOGNESE
(Cutlets, Bolognese Style)

Soak cutlets in milk for about an hour and sauté them in butter (no oil) and remove to a hot platter. Stir a generous jigger of Marsala wine and 4 tablespoons stock into the pan and simmer slightly. Cover the cutlets with grated Parmesan cheese and pour over the pan juices.

SCALOPPINE AL MARSALA *(Cutlets Marsala)*

Down around Perugia they leave off the cheese and call it simply
Scaloppine al Marsala.

SALTIMBOCCA ALLA ROMANA
(Cutlets, Roman Style)

Or do the way the Romans do. Season the cutlets with a little
sage, salt and pepper. Toothpick a slice of prosciutto or ham to
each cutlet, sauté on both sides in butter and remove to a hot
platter. Stir ½ cup dry white wine into the pan juices, simmer a
minute or two, and pour over the cutlets.

Or, place the cooked cutlets into a flameproof dish, cover with
thin slices of mozzarella cheese, and put them under the broiler
until the cheese melts. Stir 1½ cups tomato sauce into the pan
juices, spoon over the cutlets, and sprinkle with Parmesan, and
you have the famous Scaloppine di Vitello alla Parmigiana from
up Piedmont way.

If these Italians can't agree how to fix veal cutlets, how can *you*
go wrong? Fix them your own way.

How about Scaloppine Brooklyna? *You* write the recipe.

85

OSSO BUCO MILANESE *(Veal Shin, Milanese Style)*

a 3-pound veal shin, sawed into 4 lengths (be sure not to disturb the marrow)

in a heavy skillet brown the shin on all sides in the oil and butter mixture

2 tablespoons butter

2 tablespoons olive oil

salt and pepper

season with salt and pepper, place in the skillet in one layer, cut side up, toss in the vegetables and seasonings, and cook about 10 minutes

1 stalk celery, chopped

1 carrot, chopped

1 onion, chopped

blend in the flour, pour in the wine and enough stock or water to come to the top of the meat

1 sprig thyme

cover and cook slowly about 2 hours or until meat is tender

1 bay leaf

2 teaspoons flour

remove the meat, strain the sauce, and replace both in a clean pot. sprinkle with lemon peel and parsley. reheat for 2 minutes and serve

1 cup dry white wine

veal stock or water

(serves 4)

1 strip lemon peel, finely chopped

1 tablespoon parsley, finely chopped

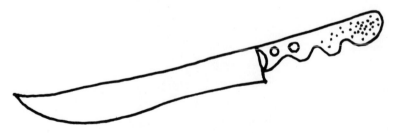

ZUPPA INGLESE *(English Cake)*

Who needs soup for dessert! Well, the Romans do, if it's "English Soup."

a sponge cake, sliced into 3 layers, about ½ an inch thick	place the bottom layer on a serving dish and pour on ½ cup rum. spread on about ½ cup jam, and ½ cup custard
1 cup some kind of jam (strawberry, raspberry, etc.)	place a second layer of cake on this and repeat with the jam and custard
1 cup prepared custard	
1 cup rum	place the third layer on top and pour on ½ cup rum, let it soak through, and top with whipped cream
3 cups whipped cream	
	(serves 8)

PESCHE AL VINO *(Peaches in Wine)*

12 fresh peach halves (or pear halves)	put the peach halves into a large pan and cover with syrup made by combining the wine, sugar, and water
1 cup wine (not too dry)	
4 tablespoons confectioners' sugar	cook slowly until tender but not soft (about 6 minutes should do it)
¼ cup water	
4 tablespoons Maraschino or rum or brandy	remove the peaches to a bowl, pour over the syrup and chill
	before serving add Maraschino
	(serves 6)

87

6

WHO
NEEDS
A
GERMAN
COOKBOOK

WHO NEEDS A GERMAN COOKBOOK

LINSENSUPPE (*Lentil Soup*)

BIERSUPPE (*Beer Soup*)

HECHT IN SAUEREN RAHM (*Pike in Sour Cream*)

FISCHROULADEN (*Fish Rolls*)

GANSELEBERSCHNITZEL (*Goose Liver Cutlet*)

SCHWEINEKOTELETTEN (*Pork Chops*)

SCHWEINEFILET (*Pork Tenderloin Fillets*)

SAUERBRATEN

SCHNITZEL

SCHNITZEL-EINTOPF (*Schnitzel Stew*)

OCHSENSCHWEIFERAGOUT (*Oxtail Ragout*)

SAUERKRAUT MIT SCHWEINKNÖCHEL
(*Sauerkraut with Pig's Knuckles*)

HASENPFEFFER (*Rabbit Stew*)

KÖNIGSBERGER KLOPSE (*Königsberg Meat Balls*)

KIRSCHPFANNKUCHEN (*Cherry Pancake*)

HEISAUFLAUF (*Rice Soufflé*)

Germany is a pork country.

Pork is to the Germans as beef is to the British. And it's been that way ever since the early days of Roman occupation when Claudius was emperor and was married to a Cologne girl named Agrippina, his niece, no less! A mosaic, which was once the floor of a Roman banquet hall in Colonia (Cologne, now), was unearthed during World War II and depicts a wild boar featured among other gastronomic delicacies of the day—oysters, songbirds, ducks. According to early Roman historians (Tacitus, for one), Germanic tribes also ate venison, rabbits, nuts, sour milk, and a variety of fruits which they often cooked with the meat. They still do. There's Birnesuppe (pear soup), fillets of sole with bananas, Rindfleisch mit Apfeln (beef with apples), Schnitzel mit Ananas (veal cutlet with pineapple), and shrimp with peaches, just to name a few.

Sauerkraut, a German standby, didn't get on the menu until the thirteenth century and potatoes, incredibly, were scarcely known until the seventeenth century when Frederick the Great introduced them from South America. In today's Germany potatoes are indispensable. They're made into dumplings, pancakes, salads, and breads. And they're baked and boiled and fried in almost countless ways.

German food is altogether exciting and distinctive: sweet salads, sour meats, fruit soups, black bread, plump sausages, all washed down with wines from the valleys of the Ruhr, Saar, Moselle, and Rhine, or with the great lager and pilsner beers from Bavaria.

91

LINSENSUPPE (*Lentil Soup*)

½ pound lentils, soaked overnight	cook the lentils in a couple quarts salted water about an hour or until soft
salt	
2 tablespoons butter	in a small skillet melt the butter, stir in the flour and about a cup of the lentil water until smooth
4 tablespoons flour	
2 strips cooked bacon or sliced frankfurters or other sausage	add this thickener, the meat, and vinegar to the soup. heat, stir, and serve with croutons
a little vinegar	(serves 4–6)
croutons	

You can make this with *Erbsen* or *Bohnen* (peas or beans, to you), as well. Season the pea soup with a little marjoram and the bean soup with a little garlic instead of the vinegar used with the lentils.

92

BIERSUPPE *(Beer Soup)*

This is a very popular soup in Bavaria. It's made with or without
sugar and with or without milk. (And ale can be substituted for
beer.) Here's the most popular recipe which includes the works.
Do it without milk and sugar, if you wish.

1 tablespoon butter	in a saucepan brown the flour and sugar in melted butter
2 tablespoons flour	
1 tablespoon sugar	add the beer, lemon juice, chopped lemon peel, and cinnamon and simmer a few minutes
2 bottles beer	
juice of ½ lemon	add the hot milk in which the eggs have been beaten, season to taste, and serve with toasted rye bread
lemon peel, chopped	
½ teaspoon (or 1 stick) cinnamon	(serves 4)
1 pint hot milk	
2 eggs	
salt and pepper	
rye toast	

93

HECHT IN SAUEREN RAHM (*Pike in Sour Cream*)

Here's a good typical German fish dish. If you haven't got pike, use perch or flounder or sole. It'll still be a good typical German fish dish.

2 pounds pike, cleaned and cut into pieces	in a heavy skillet melt the butter, add wine, anchovies, lemon slices, breadcrumbs, salt and pepper
4 tablespoons butter	
1 cup Rhine wine or other dry white wine	put fish in this mixture and simmer gently for about 15 minutes
2 anchovy fillets	
2 slices lemon, peeled	add the cream, bring to a boil, and serve
2 tablespoons breadcrumbs	(serves 4)
salt and pepper	
1 cup sour cream	

94

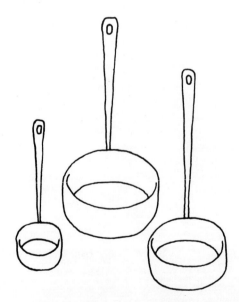

FISCHROULADEN (*Fish Rolls*)

2 *pounds fish fillets* (*sole or flounder*)	sprinkle fillets with lemon juice and a little salt
lemon juice	in a heavy skillet brown the onions with the bacon, add
salt	the pickles and parsley, and make a thick mixture
1 *onion, chopped*	
2 *slices bacon*	cover the fillets with the pickle mixture, roll and tie with string or fasten with
1 *cup pickles* (**not too sweet**), *chopped*	toothpicks
1 *tablespoon parsley, chopped*	roll in the flour-breadcrumbs and sauté in butter until golden
flour and breadcrumbs	(serves 4)
5 *tablespoons butter*	

GANSELEBERSCHNITZEL (*Goose Liver Cutlet*)

1 *goose liver* (*or 4 chicken livers*) *sliced* ½ *inch thick*	sprinkle the liver slices with paprika, flour, salt and pepper and sauté in butter until golden. remove to a warm platter
paprika	
flour	
salt and pepper	pour the wine into the pan just used and thicken with a little flour
2 *tablespoons butter*	
¾ *cup sweet wine* (*port or Madeira*)	pour over the liver slices and garnish with the grapes
1 *cup seedless grapes, sliced*	(serves 2)

95

An apple, peeled and chopped and fried in oil with chopped onion, can be used as a garnish in place of the grapes.

SCHWEINEKOTELETTEN *(Pork Chops)*

Who needs a cookbook for pork chops. Even in Germany they merely heat a skillet, throw in the chops, and cook until crisp. (Sometimes they use butter.)

When they get tired of eating pork chops *naturel,* the Germans season them, dip them in eggs and breadcrumbs, and fry in butter or fat.

Or sometimes they spread the chops with mustard (or with a horseradish-vinegar paste), brown them in butter, and stew them in beef stock or white wine.

Sometimes chopped onions or tomato sauce get into the act— and often fried sliced apples. (Bet you could even use pineapples or cranberries.)

In Germany—just like here—if they want a thick brown gravy, they sprinkle a little flour into the pan, stir, and thin down with water, stock, milk, or wine.

SCHWEINEFILET *(Pork Tenderloin Fillets)*

96

1½ pounds pork tenderloin cut into ¾-inch fillets	season the fillets and sauté them with the onion and tomato in butter, using a heavy skillet
salt and pepper	
2 tablespoons butter	cut the heat, cover and simmer gently for a half hour, and remove to a warm platter
1 onion, sliced	
1 tomato, chopped	to the skillet add flour, stir and thin down with stock. then add a tablespoon sour cream and enough white wine to make a smooth, semithick sauce
1 tablespoon flour	
¼ cup beef stock	
1 tablespoon sour cream	
white wine	pour over the fillets and serve
	(serves 4)

SAUERBRATEN

2 cups wine vinegar	heat the vinegar and water, add the onion, bay leaf, cloves, peppercorns, and sugar. boil slightly and cool
2 cups water	
1 onion, sliced	
1 bay leaf	season the meat well with salt and pepper, place in a bowl, and cover with the marinade. cover and refrigerate for 24 hours or longer
2 cloves	
10 peppercorns	
¼ cup sugar	remove the meat and wipe it dry (save the marinade)
4 pounds boneless beef (chuck roast, rump roast, shoulder)	dredge the meat well with flour and brown on all sides in bacon fat, using a heavy pot. add 2 cups of the marinade, cover and stew slowly (turning) for 2–3 hours or until meat is tender
salt and pepper	
flour	
2 tablespoons bacon fat	remove the meat to a hot platter and carve
flour (again)	
2 cups sour cream	thicken the gravy with a little flour mixed with water, stir in the sour cream, and pour over the meat or serve separately
	(serves 8)

97

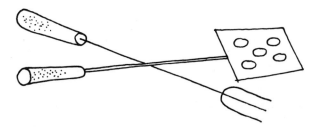

SCHNITZEL

The basic method of cooking Schnitzel all over central Europe is given below. When the Germans get tired of eating veal this way, they top the cutlets with crossed anchovy fillets and a fried egg (Schnitzel à la Holstein). Or they dip them in egg and bread-crumbs before frying. Or they simmer them in Rhine wine and season with paprika. Or sometimes a sour-cream sauce is added.

1½ pounds boneless veal, sliced into 4 ½-inch cutlets	pound the cutlets lightly until very thin and soak in milk for 10 minutes
milk	
salt and pepper	season with salt and pepper, brush with oil, and sauté slowly in butter on both sides until brown and crisp (about 20 minutes)
olive oil	
2 tablespoons butter	
chopped parsley	garnish with chopped parsley and lemon slice
sliced lemon	(serves 4)

98

SCHNITZEL-EINTOPF *(Schnitzel Stew)*

1½ pounds beef (round or chuck) cut into cubes ½ inch thick

1 onion, chopped

4 tablespoons olive oil

2 carrots, sliced

3 potatoes, peeled and sliced

1½ cups beef stock

salt and pepper

½ cup cream

2 tablespoons catsup

1 tablespoon flour

chopped parsley

brown meat and onion in oil, using a heavy skillet

add the carrots, potatoes, beef stock, salt and pepper, cover and simmer 30 minutes or until everything is done

mix the cream, catsup, and flour and add to the stew

simmer a few minutes and serve garnished with parsley

(serves 4)

99

OCHSENSCHWEIFERAGOUT (*Oxtail Ragout*)

3 pounds oxtail, disjointed	dredge the oxtail in flour seasoned with salt and pepper and brown in oil in a heavy skillet
flour	
salt and pepper	
3 tablespoons oil	add the wine and beef stock and all the other ingredients, cover and stew 2–3 hours or until meat is tender
1 cup dry red wine	
2 cups beef stock or bouillon	(serves 4)
a few vegetables such as sliced onions, tomatoes, celery, etc.	
1 bay leaf	
2 whole cloves	
1 pinch thyme	

SAUERKRAUT MIT SCHWEINKNÖCHEL
(*Sauerkraut with Pig's Knuckles*)

4 fresh pig's knuckles	scrub the pig's knuckles, place with the sauerkraut into a heavy pot, sprinkle with caraway seeds and onion, and cover with wine
1 quart sauerkraut, packaged or canned	
1 tablespoon caraway seeds	
1 onion, chopped	cover the pot and simmer 3 or 4 hours or until the knuckles are well done
Rhine wine or other dry white wine	(serves 4)

100

Just before serving you can add ½ cup sour cream, a cup of chopped boiled potatoes, or a cup of chopped frankfurters. Or, if you don't like pig's knuckles and sauerkraut, you can throw the whole mess out the window.

HASENPFEFFER (*Rabbit Stew*)

Rabbit is not always available in its fur coat around these parts, but it comes in packages, frozen, and is just as good. But it still needs marinating.

½ cup wine vinegar

make a marinade by mixing the steeping ingredients together

½ cup water

1 cup red wine

defrost the rabbit, cut it into serving pieces, cover it with the marinade, and refrigerate 24 hours

1 onion, sliced

1 teaspoon dry mustard

remove the rabbit pieces, dry well, dust with flour, and brown in the butter, using a heavy skillet

2 whole cloves

1 teaspoon freshly ground pepper

add 1 cup of the marinade (strained), cover and stew about 1½ hours or until tender

2 teaspoons salt

1 bay leaf

remove the rabbit to a heated platter, stir the sugar and sour cream into the sauce, thicken with flour if necessary, check the seasoning, pour over the rabbit and serve

1 package frozen rabbit (about 2 pounds)

4 tablespoons flour

4 tablespoons butter

(serves 4)

101

½ tablespoon sugar

½ cup sour cream

flour

KÖNIGSBERGER KLOPSE (*Königsberg Meat Balls*)

2 large, unsweetened rolls

1 pound ground meat
(½ beef, ½ pork)

3 or 4 anchovies, chopped

1 onion, chopped

2 eggs

salt and pepper

flour

2 tablespoons butter

1 tablespoon flour

1 cup beef stock

½ cup dry white wine

2 or 3 chopped anchovies

juice of ½ lemon

1 teaspoon capers

soak the rolls in milk or water, and squeeze them dry. mix with the meat, anchovies, onion, eggs, salt and pepper. knead well and shape into 8 balls

coat the *Klopse* with flour, drop them into boiling salted water, and simmer about 10 minutes

meanwhile, in a large skillet melt the butter, mix in the flour, stir, add the stock and wine, stir, add the remaining ingredients and simmer for 10 minutes

add the *Klopse* to the sauce, simmer a couple of minutes and serve

(serves 4)

KIRSCHPFANNKUCHEN *(Cherry Pancakes)*

4 large, unsweetened rolls	tear up the rolls, soak them in milk, and mix thoroughly with flour, eggs, and sugar
1 cup milk	
4 tablespoons flour	defrost (or de-pit) cherries and fold into the roll mixture
2 eggs	
2 teaspoons sugar	drop spoonfuls into a hot buttered skillet and sauté until golden
1 package frozen cherries or 1 pound fresh cherries	
	serve, garnished with cinnamon-sugar
butter	(serves 4)
cinnamon and powdered sugar	

The Kirschpfannkuchen can be served as a dessert topped with whipped cream, or flambéd with a jigger of kirsch or brandy.

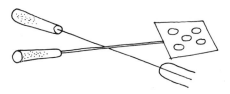

103

REISAUFLAUF *(Rice Soufflé)*

1 cup rice	cook the rice according to the directions on the package, drain, add hot milk and salt. simmer about 10 minutes and cool
2½ cups hot milk	
½ teaspoon salt	
3 tablespoons butter	meanwhile, cream the butter with the sugar and lemon peel and mix in the vanilla and egg yolks
3 tablespoons confectioners' sugar	
1 teaspoon grated lemon peel	add the rice and fold in the beaten egg whites, pour into a well-buttered baking dish, dot with butter, and bake for a half hour in a hot oven (about 400°)
½ teaspoon vanilla	
3 egg yolks	
3 egg whites, beaten	garnish with ground nutmeg and serve topped with whipped cream
butter	
ground nutmeg	(serves 4)
whipped cream	

Before you add the rice, throw in a couple tablespoons raisins. Or try thinly sliced apples (about ½ cup) or cherries or ½ pound cream cheese or a couple tablespoons strawberry jam (or some other kind of jam) or a couple tablespoons sliced almonds or caraway seeds.

104

7

WHO
NEEDS
AN
ENGLISH
COOKBOOK

WHO NEEDS AN ENGLISH COOKBOOK

THE ENGLISH BREAKFAST

BLOATERS AND KIPPERS

KEDGEREE

KIDNEYS

SARDINE TOAST

GRILLED ANCHOVY SNACKS

HAM CROÛTES

MULLIGATAWNY SOUP

COCK-A-LEEKIE

WHITEBAIT

FISH PIE

DEVILED ROAST BEEF BONES

ROAST BEEF WITH YORKSHIRE PUDDING

LANCASHIRE HOT-POT

PORK PIE

BOILED MUTTON WITH CAPER SAUCE

TEA SCONES

TRIFLE

106

Did you know that it takes the average human stomach six hours to digest a piece of boiled salted beef and only half that time for roast beef? And that roast pork takes five hours and fifteen minutes, while boiled mutton takes only three hours—and boiled tripe only an hour?

This bit of information was supplied by *Mrs. Beeton's Book of Household Management,* a four-inch-thick volume that has been a household word among British housewives since 1861. Since roast beef, boiled mutton, and tripe are great gastronomic favorites in England, Mrs. Beeton may well have provided the answer to why English cooking is the way it is—"plain" and "wholesome."

Although Mrs. Beeton focuses her attention on all manners of household chores (the engaging and wages of servants, how to make poultices and medicines in your own kitchen, the rearing and management of infants and children), more than 1,573 pages are devoted to cookery.

Who needs a cookbook in England.

Maybe it's true what they say about the fare in England being "simple" and "wholesome," leaning heavily on the primitive methods of merely applying fire to food. A French cook applying for a job in an English household was asked whether she was familiar with the art of British cooking. "Oui, Madame," she replied, "it is very easy—you just put things in hot water and take them out again after a little while."

Don't jump to any quick conclusions, though. It's not all that easy. Even simple cooking requires know-how, care, finesse—and love.

107

THE ENGLISH BREAKFAST

The English like to eat breakfast, and although it has suffered some shortcuts during the hustle of modern-day living, it is still their favorite meal. And what a variety of dishes they have to choose from: fresh grilled herrings, fried sole or plaice, kippers or bloaters, sausages, bacon and eggs, grilled kidneys, kedgeree, porridge, toast, breakfast scones, marmalade, stewed fruit, and a choice of tea or coffee.

Here are a few of the favorites:

BLOATERS AND KIPPERS

A bloater is a herring that has been caught close enough to the shore to be brought in and cured (smoked) while still fresh. A kipper is a little different. Catch the herring, split it, salt it down while still at sea, bring it in and smoke it, and you have a kipper. Kippers keep longer.

Both are delicious brushed with melted butter or oil and cooked under the broiler or in a skillet. But first they should be soaked in hot water for a few minutes (or for an hour if they seem dry or oversmoked) and then wiped dry.

KEDGEREE

108

English Kedgeree is a very bland version of an Indian dish and here's how you make it. Cook ½ cup rice, drain it, and dry it (over very slow heat). Melt 4 tablespoons butter, add the rice, season with salt, pepper, and cayenne. Then add ½ pound cooked dried fish (haddock or herring, or you can use canned salmon) that has been skinned, boned, and flaked, and the chopped whites of 2 hard-cooked eggs. Stir, heat, and serve stacked into a pyramid and decorated with chopped egg yolks.

KIDNEYS

Remove the fat and skin and split the kidneys lengthwise but not all the way. Run a skewer through them to keep them open, brush them with oil or butter, season with salt and pepper, and cook under a broiler or in a skillet. Serve on hot buttered toast.

Pubs are an important part of English life and many of them serve excellent snacks.

SARDINE TOAST

2 cans skinned and boned sardines	chop the sardines and cook a few minutes in the butter and milk
1 tablespoon butter	
2 tablespoons milk	add the egg yolks, season well with cayenne, stir, and pour onto hot buttered toast squares
2 egg yolks	
cayenne	(serves 4)
toast squares, buttered	

GRILLED ANCHOVY SNACKS

109

2 cans anchovy fillets	cut the anchovies into small pieces and grind them with the oil in a mortar with the parsley and garlic
2 tablespoons chopped parsley	
1 clove garlic, crushed	
toast squares, buttered	spread on hot buttered toast squares, dot with butter, and put under broiler. serve hot
	(serves 4)

HAM CROÛTES

1 cup finely chopped ham

2 tablespoons finely chopped shallots or scallions

1 teaspoon chopped parsley

1 tablespoon cream

2 egg yolks

salt

cayenne

bread slices fried in butter

mix all the ingredients except the bread slices and stir over slow heat

season well with cayenne and when mixture has thickened spread on hot buttered toast squares or croûtes of fresh bread

(serves 4)

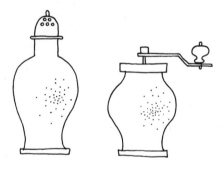

110

MULLIGATAWNY SOUP

2 pounds mutton or lamb, cut into cubes	remove the fat from the meat and melt it in a large, heavy saucepan or pot
2 tablespoons flour	dredge the meat in a mixture of the flour, curry, and salt and brown it lightly in the fat
1 tablespoon curry powder	
1 teaspoon salt	
2 onions, sliced	toss in the vegetables and apples, and any of the flour mixture that might be left and cook for 15 minutes
2 carrots, sliced	
2 apples, peeled and sliced	add the *bouquet,* pour in the hot water, cover and cook for 3 hours. skim the scum that rises to the top
1 small turnip, sliced	
1 bouquet garni (*parsley, thyme, bay leaf*)	strain, run the meat through a wire sieve, and return it to the soup
2 quarts hot water	
the juice of ½ lemon	add the lemon juice, season, and simmer a few minutes
salt and pepper	(serves 6)

111

COCK-A-LEEKIE

This is a Scotch soup. It's very old. There are many ideas of how it should be made, but the following recipe is regarded as the genuine Scotch version. Leave out the prunes, if you wish. Many Scots do.

1 cock (or small stewing chicken)	tie up the chicken and put it with the leeks into a heavy pot or saucepan, cover with stock or stock plus water
2 bunches leeks (the white parts only), cut into 1-inch pieces	
veal, beef, or chicken stock	bring to a boil, skim the scum, season with salt and pepper, cover and simmer about 3 hours or until the chicken is tender
salt and pepper	
dozen prunes	about a half hour before serving add the prunes (this is up to you)
	carve the chicken into small pieces, put them into a soup tureen, pour the soup over them, and serve
	(serves 6)

112

WHITEBAIT

Whitebait, the small fry of the herring and sprat, appear off the coast of the British Isles in large shoals nearly all year round and they are a great delicacy. To cook them you put flour in a paper bag, toss in the whitebait, and shake until the fish are well coated. Then you shake off the excess flour, put them in a frying basket and plunge them into very hot oil for 2–3 minutes. That's it.

You eat them with a little salt, perhaps a little cayenne, and a squeeze of lemon.

FISH PIE

3 cups leftover fish, skinned, boned, and chopped	mix the fish, suet, potatoes, eggs, salt and pepper with enough milk to make a stiff batter
½ cup suet, finely chopped	
½ cup leftover mashed potatoes	put the mixture into a well-buttered casserole or baking dish, sprinkle with breadcrumbs, dot with butter, and bake in a moderate oven for about 45 minutes
2 eggs	
½ teaspoon salt	
pepper	serve from the casserole
about a cup milk	(serves 4)
½ cup breadcrumbs	
butter	

DEVILED ROAST BEEF BONES

4 freshly roasted rib bones	trim some of the fat from the rib bones and sprinkle with salt and pepper
salt and pepper	
2 tablespoons English mustard	make a thin paste with the mustard and cream and coat the bones generously on all sides
3 tablespoons cream	
2 cups breadcrumbs	sprinkle with breadcrumbs, dab with melted butter, and place under the broiler until crisp, brown, and crusty
4 tablespoons melted butter	
	(serves 2–4, depending)

113

ROAST BEEF WITH YORKSHIRE PUDDING

Roast beef is England. England is roast beef. From the early days of the great joint on the spit and kings with greasy fingers gnawing on beef bones, British appetites have never wavered when roast beef was on the table. And likely as not, there was a little Yorkshire Pudding along with it.

This ingenious excuse for mopping up gravy originated when a pan of batter was placed under the roasting rack to catch the drippings.

Today the beef is roasted at a temperature too low to produce a good crisp Yorkshire Pudding, so the two are cooked separately.

First, you make the pudding, and here's how:

½ cup flour	sift together the flour and salt, gradually add the milk,
½ teaspoon salt	stirring until smooth
½ cup milk	beat in the eggs and add ½ cup water and beat
2 eggs, beaten until fluffy	vigorously, or use a blender
½ cup water	put aside

Second, you cook the roast, and here's a good way to do it:

Take a 6-pound rib roast (with short ribs removed) and season it, if you like, by rubbing with cut onion or cut garlic. Preheat the oven to 525°, stand the roast fat side up on a greased rack placed over a shallow roasting pan, slide it into the oven, turn the heat down to 350°—and walk away. (Do not salt, do not baste, do not poke with a fork.)

Get out your computer and calculate 16 minutes per pound for rare, or 22 minutes per pound for medium. (If you like it well done, go to the nearest psychoanalyst and have your head inspected.)

When the roast is done to your taste, remove it to a heated platter or carving board and sprinkle with salt and freshly ground pepper.

114

Third, turn the oven up to 400°, heat a 9 x 10 baking dish or pan, pour about ¼ inch of beef drippings into the bottom and let it get smoking hot.

Take the batter, beat it a little, and pour it into the baking dish and bake it for 20 minutes. Reduce the oven temperature to 350° and continue baking for 15 minutes longer.

Cut the Yorkshire Pudding into squares, carve the roast into thin slices (if you're English—thick slabs if you're American), and serve the two together.

(Serves 6–8)

LANCASHIRE HOT-POT

2 pounds boneless mutton or lamb, cut into 1-inch cubes	in a large casserole brown the meat on all sides
5 potatoes, peeled and thinly sliced	arrange layers of meat, onions, and potatoes in the pot, season with salt and pepper,
2 onions, sliced	and repeat. top layer should be potatoes
2 teaspoons salt	
freshly ground pepper	pour in the beef stock, cover and bake at 350° for 2 hours or until meat is tender.
2 cups hot beef stock thickened with a tablespoon flour	remove cover during last half hour to brown the potatoes
	(serves 6)

115

You can add sliced carrots, sliced mushrooms, sliced lamb kidneys, oysters, and even paprika and nobody in Lancashire will get mad at you. You could even get away with beef in place of lamb or mutton.

PORK PIE

2 pounds lean, boneless pork, cut into 1-inch cubes

put the meat into a saucepan, bring to a boil, and skim the scum

2 onions, sliced

1 cup beef or veal stock

add the onion and stock, season with salt and pepper and sage, cover and simmer 2 hours or until meat is tender

salt

freshly ground pepper

make pie dough according to the directions on the package and use it to line a buttered round or oval oven dish

pinch sage

1 package piecrust

1 tablespoon butter

pour in the meat and gravy and add the hard-cooked eggs

2 hard-cooked eggs, sliced

white of an egg

cover with a lid of pie dough, press down the edges, brush top with egg white, and perforate to allow steam to escape

bake in a preheated oven at 300° until golden. serve hot or cold

(serves 4)

116

BOILED MUTTON WITH CAPER SAUCE

5-pound leg of mutton (or lamb)

place meat into a large pot, cover with boiling water, and simmer for an hour

6 onions, halved

6 carrots, halved

skim the scum, add the vegetables and seasonings. cover and simmer for an hour longer or until meat is tender

6 leeks, halved

3 stalks celery

set aside and skim again

2 cloves garlic, cut

1 tablespoon salt

1 teaspoon whole peppercorns

4 tablespoons flour

4 tablespoons capers

in a small saucepan combine 4 tablespoons of this fat with 4 tablespoons of flour, stir for a few minutes, and add 3 cups of the broth, a little salt, and the capers. cook, stirring, until the sauce is well blended and slightly thick

serve the meat, surrounded by vegetables, on a large platter. serve the caper sauce separately

(serves about 6)

117

TEA SCONES

2 cups flour	in a mixing bowl combine the flour, salt, baking powder, and sugar, cut in the shortening (using a pastry blender) and the raisins
½ teaspoon salt	
2½ teaspoons baking powder	
¼ cup confectioners' sugar	lightly beat an egg with the milk, add to the dry mixture, and stir with a fork until the dough is uniform
⅓ cup shortening	
½ cup dried raisins	place dough onto a lightly floured board, knead gently (about 12 strokes), roll out to ¼ inch thick, and cut into rounds with a biscuit cutter
1 egg	
½ cup milk	place scones onto a baking sheet about one inch apart and bake in a preheated 425° oven for 12 to 15 minutes
	split, butter, and serve while hot
	(makes about a dozen scones)

Leave out the sugar and you have breakfast scones.

118

TRIFLE

2 sponge cupcakes, sliced in half	arrange the cupcake halves in a deep dish or bowl and sprinkle with crumbled macaroons
4 macaroons, crumbled	
½ cup sweet sherry	pour on the sherry and brandy and allow to soak for 15 minutes
2 tablespoons brandy	
1 cup raspberry or strawberry jam	spread thickly with jam, cover with whipped cream, and decorate with sliced almonds
1 cup sweetened whipped cream	(serves 4)
¼ cup sliced almonds	

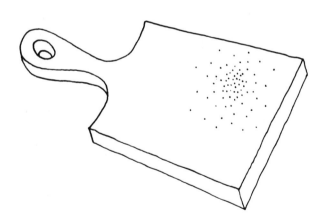

8

WHO
NEEDS
A
SPANISH
COOKBOOK

WHO NEEDS A SPANISH COOKBOOK

BOLAS DE QUESO (*Cheese Balls*)

PEPITAS CON CURRY (*Curried Pumpkin Seeds*)

GAMBAS AL AJILLO (*Shrimp with Garlic*)

SARDINAS EN CAZUELA (*Sardines in Casserole*)

BUÑUELITOS DE JAMÓN (*Ham Fritters*)

GAZPACHO

SOPA DE AJO (*Garlic Soup*)

SOPA DE PESCADO (*Fish Soup*)

HUEVOS AL PLATO (*Shirred Eggs*)

HUEVOS À LA FLAMENCA (*Eggs Flamenco*)

CACEROLA DE MARISCOS (*Seafood Casserole*)

MERO KOSKERA (*Halibut, Basque Style*)

MERO AL JEREZ (*Halibut with Sherry*)

COCHINILLO ASADO À LA CASTELLANA
(*Roast Suckling Pig, Castilian Style*)

PAELLA

RIÑÓNES À LA CASTELLANA (*Kidneys, Castilian Style*)

CREMA DE MÁLAGA (*Málaga Cream*)

AMOR FRÍO (*Cold Love—Spanish Cream, to you*)

Spain is one of the most mountainous countries of Europe. It also has a very long seacoast bordering on both the Atlantic Ocean and the Mediterranean Sea, and great areas of flat plains. All these factors combine to split Spain into a number of almost unrelated regions: the Basque country in the north, Andalusia in the south, the Costa Brava along the eastern coast, the central Castilian plains. . . .

These mountain people, fishermen, and plainsmen grow different foods, make different wines, and have different gastronomic tastes. They even speak different languages or dialects. Who needs a cookbook in Spain.

But these people have one very curious taste in common: they like their food young. Lamb is slaughtered when only twenty-six days old and a leg of lamb is served as an individual portion, no larger than a turkey drumstick. (An entire suckling lamb will provide only about 6 servings.) Suckling pigs (almost a rarity in the United States) appear on most restaurant menus throughout Spain, and are a common sight in all markets. Pork chops are served by the dozen.

And then there are baby eels—a great Spanish delicacy. Served in a dish with a little garlic these eels, no longer than three inches, look exactly like spaghetti. But that isn't all. There are tiny squid, sardines no longer than your thumbnail, and crabs the size of a silver dollar.

With all the pork, lamb, veal, seafood, fresh vegetables, and rice the Spanish have an abundance of food and they seem to be eating all the time.

Yet, in Spain it's a long time between meals. Breakfast is early and light—and lunch, the main meal of the day, though heavy, is not served until two. And what's worse, dinner or supper doesn't come until ten at night at the earliest.

123

The answer: a constant round of between-meal snacks—or *tapas*—morning, afternoon, and evening. *Tapas* are "lids" or "covers"—pieces of bread you used to put on your sherry glass to keep the flies out. Nowadays *tapas* are covered with chicken salad, shrimp, sardines, sausages, infant eels, or any of a million other goodies and they are eaten with sherry, beer, a small cup of thick hot chocolate or bitter coffee.

A few you can make (to keep the flies out of your martini) are given on the following pages.

BOLAS DE QUESO *(Cheese Balls)*

½ pound some kind of soft cheese (or grated hard cheese)

¾ cup flour

4 tablespoons butter

breadcrumbs

mix the cheese, flour, and butter, form into small balls, and roll them into breadcrumbs

place on foil or in a pie pan and bake in a 350° oven until golden. serve hot

(serves about 6)

PEPITAS CON CURRY *(Curried Pumpkin Seeds)*

¼ cup curry powder

¼ cup warm water

1 clove garlic, crushed

2 teaspoons lemon juice

1 teaspoon salt

2 cups hulled pumpkin seeds

butter

mix the curry, ¼ cup warm water, garlic, lemon juice, and salt into a small saucepan, add a cup water, and simmer a few minutes, stirring

add the pumpkin seeds, simmer a minute or so, remove, and drain

place on a cookie sheet or in a pie pan, dot with butter, and toast in the oven until crisp

124

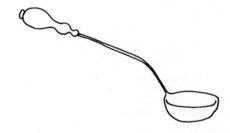

GAMBAS AL AJILLO *(Shrimp with Garlic)*

1 pound small raw shrimp in shell	shell the shrimp, leaving on the tails for handles
½ cup olive oil	in a small casserole heat the oil and garlic, toss in the
2 cloves garlic, crushed	shrimp, and cook until pink
1 tablespoon minced parsley	remove, sprinkle with parsley, and serve
dash of salt	(serves about 4)

Or set up a hibachi on the table in your backyard, grab the shrimp by the tail, dip him in hot oil, and wash him down with beer or a glass of cold dry white wine.

SARDINAS EN CAZUELA *(Sardines in Casserole)*

2 cans small sardines	arrange the sardines, each covered with a pimiento strip in the bottom of a shallow casserole
1 can pimientos, cut into strips the size of the sardines	
½ cup olive oil	cover with oil and finely chopped onion, and sprinkle lightly with salt
onion, finely chopped	
salt	bake in a 300° oven for 20 or 30 minutes
toast strips	place the sardines and pimientos on toast strips and spoon a little of the sauce over each
	(serves about 4)

125

BUÑUELITOS DE JAMÓN *(Ham Fritters)*

2 egg yolks, beaten	mix the beaten egg yolks, flour, cream, ham, and seasonings
2 tablespoons flour	
2 tablespoons cream, sweet or sour	fold in the egg whites
2 cups ground ham	heat the olive oil in a small skillet. drop spoonfuls of the mixture into the hot oil and cook until golden on all sides. serve hot
salt and pepper	
pinch cayenne	(serves about 6)
2 egg whites, beaten until stiff	
olive oil	

Substitute crisp bacon or finely chopped sausage for the ham. Add a little garlic or a pinch of curry or chili powder.

GAZPACHO

Gazpacho is a very old dish (only recently discovered by Americans) served all over Spain—in the mountains, in the plains, on the seacoast, in the cities, and in the rural areas where it originated. (And Mexicans love it, too.) It's eaten as a liquid salad, a cold soup, or a refreshing one-dish luncheon after a hot morning in the fields.

Like chowder in the United States and minestrone in Italy, Gazpacho can be prepared in a seemingly limitless variety of ways. You don't need a cookbook; all you need is tomatoes, garlic, vinegar, and olive oil—and a little ingenuity. If you are a Spanish peasant, you'll throw in some breadcrumbs. Any other ingredients you care to include will only add to the excitement of the dish. Just one other thing, a blender—used today by many Spaniards —will help enormously.

8 fresh ripe tomatoes, peeled and seeded, or one large can tomatoes or 2 cups tomato puree

2 or 3 cloves garlic, crushed

¼ cup good olive oil

1 or 2 tablespoons wine vinegar

1 teaspoon salt

2 cups chicken broth, or water

1 cucumber, peeled and chopped (optional but desirable)

1 cup breadcrumbs (optional but desirable)

1 pimiento (optional)

¼ teaspoon cumin (optional)

dash Tabasco or cayenne (optional)

put everything into a blender and beat until smooth. chill thoroughly and put into a soup plate with an ice cube in the center

serve garnished with minced scallions and green peppers, chopped black olives, chopped green peppers, and/or breadcrumbs sautéed in olive oil

(serves about 8)

127

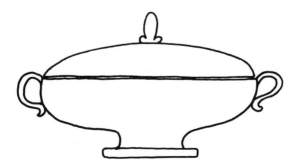

SOPA DE AJO *(Garlic Soup)*

4 tablespoons olive oil	heat the olive oil in a saucepan, add the garlic and bread, and sauté gently until the bread is golden (do not burn)
6 cloves garlic, peeled	
6 slices Italian or French bread cut into cubes	
1 medium can tomatoes, sieved, or 1 cup tomato puree	discard the garlic, remove the bread and mash to a paste and put into a saucepan with the tomatoes, bay leaf, paprika, and chicken stock
½ bay leaf	
2 teaspoons paprika	simmer 10 or 15 minutes, season to taste and gradually stir in the egg yolks and then the egg whites
3 cups chicken stock	
salt and pepper	
4 egg yolks	serve garnished with minced parsley
4 egg whites	(serves 6)
minced parsley	

128

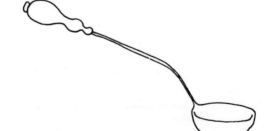

SOPA DE PESCADO *(Fish Soup)*

1 pound some kind of fish fillets	break the fillets into bits, dredge in flour, and brown in oil. then throw in the garlic, tomatoes, parsley, and seasonings
¼ cup flour	
¼ cup olive oil	simmer for 5 minutes and thin down with about 8 cups boiling water
2 cloves garlic, crushed	
2 tomatoes, diced	add the remaining ingredients and cook, stirring, about half an hour
1 tablespoon chopped parsley	
a dash Tabasco or cayenne	(serves 6)
1 teaspoon salt	
boiling water	
2 cups dry breadcrumbs	
½ cup chopped almonds	
½ cup chopped olives	

HUEVOS AL PLATO *(Shirred Eggs)*

2 tablespoons minced onion	sauté the onion and ham in oil and spoon into 2 shirring dishes or pans
4 tablespoons chopped ham	
2 tablespoons olive oil (or olive oil and butter)	break 2 eggs into each dish, season with salt and pepper, and bake in a preheated 425° oven until whites are set
4 eggs	
salt and pepper	(serves 2)

129

HUEVOS À LA FLAMENCA *(Eggs Flamenco)*

4 tablespoons chopped onion

1 clove garlic, crushed

2 tablespoons olive oil

1 cup some kind of sausage or ham, diced

1 teaspoon minced parsley

2 pimientos (canned), minced

2 tomatoes, peeled and diced

½ cup chicken stock

salt and pepper

8 eggs

using a small saucepan, sauté the onion and garlic in the oil, add the sausage or ham, and brown

add the parsley, pimientos, tomatoes, chicken stock, and salt and pepper. simmer 5 minutes

spoon the sauce into 4 shirring dishes or pans, break 2 eggs into each and bake in a preheated 425° oven until whites of eggs are set

(serves 4)

You can add cooked peas, carrots, or asparagus before putting into the oven.

130

CACEROLA DE MARISCOS *(Shellfish Casserole)*

This is sort of a Catalonian version of Bouillabaisse. It's one of those things that varies from region to region. Feel free to make any substitutions you care to.

4 tablespoons olive oil	in a heavy skillet or pot heat the oil, add the onion, pimiento, garlic. sauté gently for a few minutes
chopped onion	
chopped pimiento	
2 cloves garlic, crushed	dredge the fish in flour, add to the pot, and cook until golden. then add the shrimp (or scallops) and cook until pink
1 pound some kind of fish fillets, cut into chunks	
1 pound shelled raw shrimp or scallops	toss in the tomatoes and mussels or clams (that have been well scrubbed), add the wine, and sprinkle with salt, parsley, and almonds. cook until mussel shells open
1 cup canned tomatoes	
1 quart mussels in shell or clams in shell	transfer the stew to a casserole, ignite the brandy, and pour on top. serve at once
½ cup dry white wine	
salt	(serves 4–6)
minced parsley	
2 tablespoons chopped almonds	
2 tablespoons brandy	

131

MERO KOSKERA *(Halibut, Basque Style)*

2 pounds halibut (or some other fish steaks)	marinate the fish in the oil and lemon for an hour or so, drain, and dry
¼ cup olive oil	
½ teaspoon lemon juice	dust the fish lightly with flour, season with salt, and using some of the marinade, sauté with the garlic in a heavy skillet until golden on both sides
¼ cup flour	
salt	
2 cloves garlic, peeled	discard the garlic. thicken the oil with flour and gradually add the stock. simmer gently, covered, about 15 minutes
2 cups fish or chicken stock	
1 tablespoon minced parsley	add parsley, eggs, and vegetables and simmer 5 minutes longer
3 hard-cooked eggs, quartered	
cooked vegetables (asparagus, peas, or what have you)	(serves 4)

MERO AL JEREZ *(Halibut with Sherry)*

Here's the way you serve halibut if you come from the south of Spain instead of the Basque country.

2 pounds halibut (or some other fish steaks)	dip the fish in oil, sprinkle with salt, and place in a baking dish. sprinkle with a mixture of nuts and crumbs
½ cup olive oil	
salt	bake in a preheated 350° oven for about 20 minutes, basting several times with sherry
2 tablespoons breadcrumbs	
2 tablespoons sliced or chopped almonds	(serves 4)
½ cup sherry (not too sweet)	

COCHINILLO ASADO À LA CASTELLANA
(*Roast Suckling Pig, Castilian Style*)

a suckling pig or a 4-pound fresh ham	rub the pig (or the ham) with salt, pepper, and oil and place it in a shallow roasting pan
salt and pepper	
olive oil	mix the garlic, almonds, paprika, thyme, and parsley with enough red wine to make a paste
2 cloves garlic, mashed	
6 toasted almonds, mashed	
1 teaspoon paprika	roast the meat in a preheated 325° oven, brushing from time to time with the garlic paste as it cooks. remove when well done and serve
pinch thyme	
1 teaspoon chopped parsley	(serves 4–6)
dry red wine	

The Spanish give suckling lamb almost the same treatment. You can use a leg of lamb or a loin of pork and get interesting results.

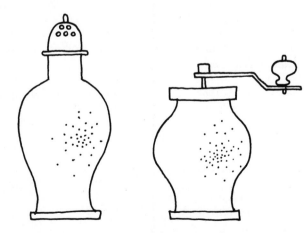

133

PAELLA

This is without a doubt the national dish of Spain. It is served everywhere throughout the country (and in Mexico, too) and there are many, many ways to make it, any one of which will start an argument with someone. Southern Spaniards say they invented the dish and that Paella à la Valenciana is the only kind fit to eat. The Catalans around Barcelona back their own version, which uses pork, less chicken, and only a suspicion of saffron.

The following is more a guide than a recipe. Stick with it and you'll produce a magnificent Paella. It might get you into arguments, but it won't lose you any friends.

some kind of meat, boned and cut into bite-size pieces: a chicken or chicken breast and/or ¼ pound lean pork and/or ¼ pound veal and/or 1 cup chopped ham or sausage

using a heavy skillet (about 10 inches) or a paella pan, if you have one, sauté the meat, onions, and garlic in the oil until crispy brown

1 onion, chopped

add the shellfish, the vegetables, saffron, and salt. cook 2 minutes, stirring

2 cloves garlic, crushed

½ cup olive oil

add the raw rice and stir well to coat the rice with oil. finally pour on the boiling water or broth, bring to a boil, and cook over moderate heat for 10 minutes. stir to prevent sticking

some shellfish:

3 lobster tails cut into pieces (shells discarded) or 1 pound of raw shelled shrimp and 12 little neck clams, scrubbed (or can minced clams) or 12 mussels, well scrubbed and/or baby squid, sliced

134

turn off the heat (or turn it to a minimum), cover and let stand 15 or 20 minutes until all the liquid has been absorbed

serve in the pan in which it was cooked

(serves 6)

some vegetables:

2 pimientos, cut into strips
and
2 tomatoes, chopped
and
½ cup frozen peas
or
½ cup chopped string beans or what have you

pinch or two or three saffron dissolved in ½ cup boiling water

2 teaspoons salt

1½ cups raw rice

3 cups boiling water or chicken broth

RIÑÓNES À LA CASTELLANA
(Kidneys, Castilian Style)

12 lamb kidneys, each cut into 4 slices	stick the kidneys and bacon pieces alternately onto skewers, brush with olive oil, season with salt and pepper, and cook under a broiler or over charcoal
8 slices bacon, each cut into 6 pieecs	
¼ cup olive oil	
salt and pepper	meanwhile, make a paste by mixing the parsley, garlic, breadcrumbs, and brandy
1 tablespoon chopped parsley	
1 clove garlic, crushed	when kidneys are half-cooked (about 4 minutes) roll in the paste, return to the grill, and cook until brown on all sides
½ cup breadcrumbs	
brandy	(serves 4)

135

CREMA DE MÁLAGA (*Málaga Cream*)

12 egg yolks	in the top pan of a double boiler beat the egg yolks and sugar
6 tablespoons sugar	
¾ cup Málaga wine	add the wine and cinnamon, continuing to beat
1 teaspoon cinnamon	
	place over hot but not boiling water, beating constantly with a wire whisk or rotary beater until mixture is thick and foamy
	serve in parfait glasses
	(serves 6)

AMOR FRÍO (*Cold Love—Spanish Cream, to you*)

1 envelope unflavored gelatin	in the top pan of a double boiler mix gelatin, sugar, salt, and cinnamon. gradually add the milk-egg mixture
¼ cup sugar	
pinch salt	
pinch cinnamon	place over hot but not boiling water and stir until custard begins to thicken. remove and chill
3 egg yolks mixed with 2 cups milk	
cup some kind of mixed fruit	meanwhile, soak the fruit and sugar in the sherry and stir into the custard
1 tablespoon confectioners' sugar	
¼ cup sweet sherry	fold in the whipped cream and then fold in the egg whites. pour into 1½-quart mold and chill until firm
½ cup heavy cream, whipped	(serves 8)
3 egg whites, beaten	

136

9

WHO
NEEDS
A
SCANDINAVIAN
COOKBOOK

WHO NEEDS A SCANDINAVIAN COOKBOOK

PICKLED HERRING

HERRING AND EGG

HERRING SALAD

GRÖNKAAL (*Cabbage Soup with Pork*)

SCANDINAVIAN FRUIT SOUP

FISKEFARCE (*Fish Mousse*)

BROILED TROUT WITH CUCUMBER

KRÄFTOR MED DILL (*Crayfish with Dill*)

ROCK CORNISH HEN IN CREAM

DYRERYG (*Reindeer*)

HÖKARPANNA (*Meat Stew*)

KÖTTBULLAR (*Swedish Meat Balls*)

KÅLDOMAR (*Stuffed Cabbage*)

BEER SOUP

GLÖGG

138

The Scandinavian countries are the land of the Smörgåsbord. In Sweden, especially, this buffet-type eating is a national institution. Served as an introduction to the main course, the Smörgåsbord is, in itself, a meal of several courses beginning unwaveringly with herring and proceeding through the fish dishes, cold cuts, and liver pâtés to the *småvarmt* ("little warm dishes" such as meat balls, kidneys, eggs, etc.). After this you are ready to sit down to dinner—meat, vegetables, salad, cheese, and dessert.

Smörgåsbord dishes are consumed in rigid sequence, always with the herring dishes first accompanied by a gulp—not a sip—of aquavit served cold but never, never diluted by ice.

The story is told of a daring young woman from Englewood, New Jersey, who, while visiting a friend in Göteborg, decided to test the sincerity of Swedish customs. She helped herself liberally to meat balls and shrimp—no herring, mind you—and returned to her place at the table, pretending to ignore the glaring look of her hostess. She then proceeded to take dainty little sips of her aquavit. Her enraged hostess, unable to contain herself at the effrontery, arose with all the dignity she could muster and asked the young American to pack up and leave at once. But the real tragedy resulted when a native guest of the party slipped out and phoned the police who arrived and apprehended the young woman just as she was leaving the house. Despite endless efforts on the part of her parents and of the United States Embassy, the young Englewood woman has never been heard from to this day.

But back to the Smörgåsbord. Many of the delicacies that go to make up a representative buffet are available in jars and tins or from the neighborhood delicatessen—sardines, smoked salmon, pickled beets, shrimp, anchovies, etc. But here are a few recipes for your special attention.

139

PICKLED HERRING

2 salt herring	clean fish, soak in cold water overnight, remove the skin and bones, and slice the fillets into ½-inch strips
1 onion, sliced into thin rings	
8–10 whole peppercorns	
2 whole cloves	arrange neatly on a shallow dish, cover with onion rings, sprinkle with peppercorns and cloves, and pour over the sugared vinegar or wine. chill in the refrigerator for 5 or 6 hours
½ cup tarragon vinegar, mixed with ½ cup sugar or ½ cup white wine with a little lemon and sugar	
	garnish with fresh dill or parsley and serve
	(serves 8)

HERRING AND EGG

To pickled herring add 4 hard-cooked eggs, chopped. Sauté a couple of minced onions gently in a couple of tablespoons of butter until golden. Add the herring and egg, mix well and heat well. Serve hot. (serves 8)

140 Take it from there and improvise your own herring dishes hot and cold. Or substitute anchovies—the smoked kind, not those canned in oil.

HERRING SALAD

Drain pickled herring and add a cup of julienne cooked meat (any kind), a cup of julienne beets, 2 cups julienne cooked potatoes, a couple of apples and cucumbers, sliced. Mix all together with a little sherry and a couple of tablespoons sour cream or mayonnaise. Chill and serve topped with hard-cooked egg slices. (serves 8)

GRÖNKAAL (*Cabbage Soup with Pork*)

2 pounds fresh lean pork, cut into 1½-inch cubes	bring the water to a boil in a large pot, add the pork, turn the heat down, and simmer for an hour. skim any fat that may rise to the top
2 quarts water	
1 cabbage	meanwhile, remove the inner leaves from a cabbage, blanch them in boiling water for 10 minutes, drain, chop, sprinkle with a little flour, and add to the soup pot along with the remaining ingredients
flour	
2 or 3 carrots, sliced	
2 leeks, sliced (or some chopped scallions)	
½ teaspoon dill	cover and continue simmering about a half hour or until meat and vegetables are tender. check seasoning
½ teaspoon tarragon	
1 bay leaf	(serves 4–6)
2 teaspoons salt	
pepper	

141

SCANDINAVIAN FRUIT SOUP

1 cup prunes (pitted)

1 cup dried apricots

1 cup dried peaches

(also dried apples or any other dried fruit, if you want)

1 teaspoon grated lemon rind

2 quarts water

½ cup sugar

2 tablespoons cornstarch

½ cup rum or sherry

salt

sour cream

place dried fruit and lemon rind in a large pot, add the water, cover, and let it soak overnight

place pot over medium heat and simmer until fruit is soft and mushy

meanwhile, mix sugar and cornstarch and make a smooth paste with the rum or sherry. stir in a little of the liquid, then add to the soup with a little salt

simmer about 5 minutes or until thickened. serve hot or cold topped with sour cream

(serves 4–6)

142

FISKEFARCE (*Fish Mousse*)

Fiskefarce in Norway, *Fiskfärs* in Sweden, *FiskeFars* in Denmark—popular in all Scandinavian countries, it can be used for making fish balls (by poaching in water or fish stock), for making fish pudding (by baking in a moderate oven) or for a variety of other dishes.

Fish Balls: Poach in water or fish stock, serve with minced fresh dill or parsley. *Fish Pudding:* Sprinkle with breadcrumbs and bake in a moderate oven for about a half hour, serve with sliced truffles, chopped mushrooms, and/or melted butter—or top with sour cream or lobster sauce.

2 or 2½ pounds fresh haddock or cod	remove the skin and bones from the fish and put through a grinder several times with
1 cup butter	the butter and then grind in mortar until it becomes a
4 egg yolks	smooth, creamy paste
½ cup cream	mix the egg yolks in a bowl with the cream, flour, salt
½ cup flour	and pepper, and add gradually to the fish paste,
1 tablespoon salt	blending thoroughly
½ teaspoon pepper	add the beaten egg whites and put into a buttered pie pan
4 egg whites, stiffly beaten	with breadcrumbs
breadcrumbs	place the pie pan in boiling water and steam for an hour
	the mousse can then be used in any of the various ways already mentioned
	(serves 4)

143

BROILED TROUT WITH CUCUMBER

4 fresh 1-pound brook, brown, or rainbow trout, cleaned and washed

spread the trout on both sides with mustard, place on an oiled broiler rack, and cook under moderate heat for about 7 minutes on each side, brushing frequently with cooking oil

8 teaspoons Dijon mustard

cooking oil

¼ cup butter

meanwhile, prepare maître d'hôtel butter by creaming the butter, parsley, and lemon juice

1 tablespoon minced parsley

1 tablespoon lemon juice

1 large cucumber, thinly sliced

place trout on a warm serving platter spread with the butter mixture and serve with chilled cucumber salad (made by mixing together cucumbers, sugared vinegar, salt, pepper, and dill)

1 tablespoon sugar dissolved in ½ cup vinegar

¼ teaspoon salt

(serves 4)

dash pepper

2 teaspoons minced dill or parsley

KRÄFTOR MED DILL *(Crayfish with Dill)*

144

The crayfish season in Sweden begins the first of August with celebrations everywhere. Great quantities of crayfish—and great quantities of aquavit—are consumed by one and all. There's really no special way to cook crayfish—you just boil them with a little dill in salted water and eat them cold.

If you don't happen to be in Sweden, and it isn't August, and you can't get hold of *kräftor*, use *rakor* (shrimp, to you).

ROCK CORNISH HEN IN CREAM

Up in the cold regions of Norway there's a kind of wild grouse called ptarmigan which the Norwegians love to eat covered with a cream sauce and lingonberries. In the United States you may have to wait a long time for ptarmigan to fly your way, but while you're waiting you can eat Rock Cornish hen prepared the same way. You'll not regret it.

4 small Rock Cornish hens, cleaned and trussed	in a heavy skillet sauté the hens in butter about an hour until golden brown on all sides
4 tablespoons butter	
salt and pepper	transfer the hens to a casserole; season with salt and pepper
3 tablespoons flour	
3 cups cream	to the skillet juices add the flour and gradually stir in the cream and a little salt and pepper, scraping the glaze from the bottom of the pan
salt and pepper	
4 slices crisp bacon	
preserved lingonberries	add the sauce to the Cornish hens, cover and cook in a preheated 350° oven for about an hour or until birds are tender
	garnish with bacon slices and serve with preserved lingonberries

145

DYRERYG *(Reindeer)*

2 pounds venison steak or chops	marinate the venison in enough vinegar and water to cover for several hours. dry thoroughly
vinegar and water	
2 tablespoons butter	in a heavy skillet brown the meat in the butter, season with salt and pepper, pour in the sour cream, cover and simmer for an hour or so or until meat is tender
salt and pepper	
½ pint sour cream	
	(serves 4–6)

HÖKARPANNA *(Meat Stew)*

2 pounds stewing beef (or pork chops), cut into ¼-inch slices	dredge the meat slices with flour, season with salt and pepper, and pound lightly
flour	in a skillet brown the meat with the onions in oil
salt and pepper	
2 onions, chopped	in a casserole place alternate layers of meat, kidney, and potatoes, add the skillet juices, a bay leaf, and a bottle of beer. cover tightly and bake for 1½ hours or until meat is tender
1 veal kidney, thinly sliced	
6 potatoes, peeled and thinly sliced	
1 bay leaf	(serves 4–6)
1 bottle beer	

146

KÖTTBULLAR *(Swedish Meat Balls)*

2 or 3 cups milk	beat the eggs with the milk, add the breadcrumbs, and let
1 or 2 eggs	them soak awhile
½ cup breadcrumbs	in a heavy skillet sauté the onions in oil until golden
1 onion, finely chopped	mix the meat with the
1 tablespoon oil	breadcrumbs, add the onions, season with salt and pepper,
salt and pepper	and form into small balls
½ pound beef, finely ground	add butter to the skillet and fry the meat balls until golden
½ pound veal, finely ground	brown. add a cup of boiling water and simmer for
½ pound pork, finely ground	15 minutes
4 tablespoons butter	(serves 6)
1 cup boiling water	

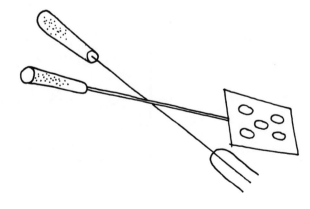

147

KÅLDOMAR (*Stuffed Cabbage*)

1 large cabbage	remove outer leaves and core from cabbage and discard. separate inner leaves and boil for 15 minutes. dry and set aside
½ cup rice	
¾ pound lean beef or veal, finely ground	
¾ pound lean pork, finely ground	boil the rice for 15 minutes in salted water. rinse and drain
1 cup water	mix the beef (or veal) with the rice. add the pork, water, eggs, salt and pepper and blend thoroughly
2 eggs	
2 teaspoons salt	place the large cabbage leaves curly edges up with a smaller leaf on top. place a spoonful of the meat mixture onto each of the smaller leaves, fold the left and right edges of the larger leaves in toward the center, and roll up from top to bottom
¼ teaspoon pepper	
1 tablespoon butter	
1 tablespoon brown sugar	
1½ cups sour cream	

arrange the cabbage rolls in the bottom of a buttered casserole, sprinkle with brown sugar, and brown in a preheated 450° oven, taking great care not to scorch

reduce the heat to 300°, baste with juices, cover and bake for 1 hour. baste again, add the sour cream, cover again, and bake for another hour

check seasoning and serve

(serves 8)

148

BEER SOUP

How mixed up can you get—a soup made of beer that's eaten as a dessert!

¼ cup flour	blend the flour with a little of the milk. add the egg and the rest of the milk and simmer for 10 minutes in a saucepan, stirring constantly
1 quart milk	
1 egg	
1 bottle beer	in another saucepan simmer the beer, molasses, and spices for a few minutes and then combine the 2 mixtures, beating rapidly with a whisk or mixer
¼ cup molasses	
pinch ginger	
6 or 8 cardamom seeds	
	serve hot in soup bowls or saucers
	(serves 4–6)

149

GLÖGG

Here is probably the greatest of all cold-weather wine punches. It's easy to make because there is so much room for improvisation. You can use almost any kind of wines in almost any proportions and quantities for it's the spicy foundation that gives Glögg its distinctive character. You can make it in advance and set it aside in a covered jar for use when you are ready (quantities suggested will yield half a dozen 4-ounce servings).

In a small saucepan place 4 or 5 whole cloves, 8 or 10 cardamom seeds, 2 sticks cinnamon, 2 cups seedless raisins, and a can of candied orange peel. Cover with some kind of wine and bring to a boil. Let it cool, put it in a jar, cover and set aside for a cold, snowy day.

On Glögg day select a nice, large pot and pour into it a bottle of sweet wine (port or muscatel, for example), a bottle of tart wine (sherry, claret, a red burgundy, etc.), ½ bottle of whiskey, brandy, or rum, ½ cup sugar, and the spicy mixture in the jar. Heat thoroughly without boiling. Ignite the fumes by tossing in a jigger of flaming brandy or whiskey. Put out the flame (by covering the pot) and serve hot in glasses containing almond slivers and raisins. Wow!

150

10

WHO
NEEDS
AN
ISRAELI
COOKBOOK

WHO NEEDS AN ISRAELI COOKBOOK

FELAFEL (*Chick-pea Tidbits*)

PITA (*Snack Pastry*)

TAHINA (*Sesame Paste*)

TUICA (*Bean Dip*)

WHOLE HOMOS (*Whole Chick-peas*)

HOMOS AND TAHINA (*Chick-pea and Sesame Paste*)

GEHAKTE LEBER (*Chopped Liver*)

PASSOVER SOUP

SCHORBAH (*Mint Soup*)

FIG SOUP

CHERRY SOUP

GEFILTE FISH

FRIED GEFILTEFISH

BOILED CARP

JEDJAD IMER (*Chicken with Honey*)

ISRAELI SOUTHERN FRIED CHICKEN, YOU-ALL

MAGUINA (*Baked Beef*)

CARNATZLACH (*Meat Balls*)

KIRSEH (*Yemenite Tripe*)

NOAH'S PUDDING

TEHAINIM MITUKIM (*Sweet Figs*)

Almost all the nations of the world have at one time or another been the uninvited guests of Palestine. From A to Z—from the Assyrians to the Zionists, and all those in between: the Babylonians, Egyptians, Greeks, Romans, Persians, and Turks, the Crusaders from England, France, Spain, and Portugal, from Holland, Belgium, and Germany—they all came to Palestine. And they all stayed for dinner.

So what kind of cooking do you find in Israel today? You name it, they've got it. You'll find the flavors of Hungary and Russia, of Italy and Spain, spices of Arabia, the fruits and nuts of the world, all served up according to Israel's own special religious requirement.

FELAFEL (*Chick-pea Tidbits*)

½ pound chick-peas, soaked overnight	mix all the ingredients and grind in a mortar, meat grinder, or blender until mealy
2 tablespoons cracked wheat, soaked two hours	
2 cloves garlic	form into small balls and fry in hot deep fat until golden brown
1 teaspoon cumin seed	
1 teaspoon salt	use as a filling for *pitas* and serve with martinis
2 tablespoons flour	
dash coriander	
dash chili powder	

153

PITA (*Snack Pastry*)

If you were a hungry, wandering desert Israelite of the early days, chances are you would mix up a dough of flour, water, and salt and you'd bake it in an earthen bowl over hot coals. The result would be *pita*. You'd eat it and you'd like it. Maybe you don't live in a desert, but in a city apartment on the twenty-seventh floor—and maybe you aren't even Jewish. You can still make *pita*—and like it. One of the things you might like about it is the way you can put *pita* to work at cocktail time.

2 packages dry yeast	stir the yeast and sugar into the water until it is dissolved. the sugar is sometimes left out
½ teaspoon sugar	
1 cup warm water	mix in the flour and salt and knead the resulting dough
4 cups flour	
1 teaspoon salt	divide the dough into 20 or 25 chunks and roll them out on a floured board until as thin as possible
	cover and place in a warm spot for half an hour until *pitas* have risen. (you may want to repeat this process to make them extra thin)
	bake the *pitas* quickly in a preheated 500° oven until they puff up
	serve them with a dip or cut them open (they're hollow, you know) and fill them with good stuff

TAHINA *(Sesame Paste)*

1 cup sesame seed	mix the sesame seeds and water together in a blender
1 cup water	
2 cloves garlic, crushed	add the remaining ingredients and continue blending. dilute with water to the texture of mayonnaise
1 teaspoon salt	
2 tablespoons lemon juice	use as a dip with *pitas* or potato chips, or spread on crackers or toast
3 tablespoons olive oil	
2 tablespoons chopped parsley	
dash cayenne	

TUICA *(Bean Dip)*

1 cup cooked navy beans	mix all the ingredients together in a blender, dilute with water if necessary, and serve as a dip with *pitas* or potato chips, or as a spread
1 clove garlic, crushed	
3 tablespoons olive oil	
1 tablespoon lemon juice	
salt and pepper	

155

WHOLE HOMOS *(Whole Chick-peas)*

Soak chick-peas overnight, change the water, and cook until tender and the skins have peeled off. Drain, cool, and season with salt, or sauté in salted butter. Serve as salted nuts.

HOMOS AND TAHINA *(Chick-pea and Sesame Paste)*

2 cups chick-peas, soaked overnight	cook the chick-peas in a little water for a couple of hours until tender and the skins begin to peel
2 cloves garlic, crushed	
1 tablespoon lemon juice	drain the chick-peas and put into a blender with the remaining ingredients. blend until the mixture becomes a smooth paste and dilute with water to the consistency of mayonnaise
dash cayenne	
salt and pepper	
1 tablespoon chopped parsley	
1 cup tahina *(see index)*	use as a dip or as a filling for *pitas*
olive oil	

GEHAKTE LEBER *(Chopped Liver)*

1 pound chicken livers	broil the livers for 2 minutes
2 large onions, chopped	in a small skillet fry the onions in the fat until golden
2 tablespoons chicken fat	
4 hard-cooked egg yolks	put the livers, onions, and egg yolks through the meat chopper, season with salt and pepper, and add the fat from the skillet
½ teaspoon salt	
dash pepper	
	(serves 4)

156

PASSOVER SOUP

This is one of those soups that never appears twice with the same ingredients. Make it your own way and it'll be just as good as you can get in Haifa or Nazareth. Or do it this way:

1 pound lamb shank, cut into pieces	in a large pot brown the lamb on all sides in olive oil
2 tablespoons olive oil	add all the vegetables and enough water to make a soup of the desired thickness
small head of cabbage, cut into pieces	
2 onions, sliced	season as desired, cover and cook about an hour
2 carrots, sliced	remove the lamb bones and serve garnished with broken matzos
1 leek, or a few scallions, chopped	
any other vegetables you have on hand	(serves 4–6)
water	
salt and pepper	
cinnamon	
cloves	
broken matzos	

157

SCHORBAH (*Mint Soup*)

1 clove garlic, crushed

2 tablespoons dried mint (or ½ cup fresh mint leaves)

2 tablespoons olive oil

2 tablespoons cornstarch dissolved in ½ cup water

2 cans chicken consommé

salt and pepper

dash cayenne

3 egg yolks, beaten

in a saucepan sauté the garlic and mint gently in oil about 10 minutes

add the cornstarch-water mixture and the consommé. stir, simmer, and season

slowly add a little of the soup to the beaten egg yolks, stirring constantly. then add the egg yolks to the soup, stir well, and serve immediately

(serves 4)

158

FIG SOUP

In a hot dry country like Israel you can understand that there is not always a roaring demand for a steaming, hearty bowl of heart-warming soup. Cold soup is popular among the Israelis. Here's a popular one—and a very, very native one.

4 cups figs, sliced	simmer the figs in the water until they're soft and mushy
4 cups water	
4 tablespoons cornstarch	add the cornstarch and continue cooking until clear
3 cups orange juice	add the orange juice, ginger, and sugar and mix well in a
pinch of ginger	blender. chill
a little sugar, if desired	serve cold topped with sour cream
sour cream	
	(serves 4–6)

Use a pound of pitted cherries instead of the figs, a little powdered cinnamon and clove instead of ginger, and a cup of red wine, and Fig Soup becomes . . .

CHERRY SOUP

159

GEFILTE FISH

Here's one of the oldest dishes in Jewish culinary history. An old *bube meinse* passed down from generation to generation to generation has it that gefilte fish was served as one of the courses of the Last Supper. Don't believe it. Old it may be, but two thousand years old it isn't—a quarter of that time is far more likely. But any dish that has been in continuous acceptance for five hundred years must be doing something right.

3 pounds fresh fish (carp, snapper, mullet, pike, etc., but at least 2 varieties)

remove the skin, head, and bones from the fish, put them in a pot with the sliced onions, sliced carrots, a teaspoon salt, ½ teaspoon pepper, and 2 cups water, and simmer for 1 hour. strain and keep the stock

3 onions, sliced

2 carrots, sliced

1 teaspoon salt

½ teaspoon pepper

meanwhile, put the fish flesh through a food chopper (several times if necessary), add grated onion, matzo meal (or bread), and eggs, chopping all the while and adding water to moisten

2 cups water

3 onions, grated

1 tablespoon matzo meal, or 2 slices dry white bread

add a tablespoon of sugar, a teaspoon of salt, and ½ teaspoon pepper (more if you want it hot). mix well and form into marble-sized balls

2 eggs

160

water

1 tablespoon sugar

bring the stock to a boil, add the fish balls, reduce the heat, cover and simmer slowly for about 2 hours

1 teaspoon salt

½ teaspoon pepper

serve cold with freshly made horseradish

(serves 8)

FRIED GEFILTE FISH

Instead of simmering the fish balls in stock, try frying them in hot olive oil until they are golden brown. Serve them hot or cold.

BOILED CARP

The Israelis like their fish fresh. According to Sholom Aleichem, the women in the marketplace are always peeking under the gills, poking at the eyes, and prodding the bellies to make sure the fish they buy are fresh. Another good way to make sure is to buy them live and keep them in a bucket of water until dinnertime. Would you believe that backyard carp ponds in Israel are as common as American suburban charcoal cook-wagons?

2 pounds fresh carp, freshly killed and cleaned

in a large pot place the vegetables, then the fish

2 onions, sliced

2 carrots, sliced

season with salt, pepper, and sugar, cover with water, and cook until fish is tender and flaky (about one half hour)

1 parsnip, sliced

3 stalks celery, chopped

remove fish to a platter, strain the sauce, and pour on. chill and serve. heat the vegetable mixture and serve separately

few peppercorns

1 tablespoon salt

161

1 tablespoon sugar

(serves 6)

water

Hungarian Jews, as you may well imagine, like to make this dish with paprika and chopped tomatoes.

JEDJAD IMER *(Chicken with Honey)*

1 roasting chicken, cleaned	rub the chicken inside and out with lemon and sprinkle with salt
1 cut lemon	
1 teaspoon salt	melt the margarine, mix with the honey, and brush onto the chicken inside and out
4 tablespoons margarine (or butter)	
4 tablespoons honey	roast in a preheated oven at 350° about 1½ hours or until tender, basting from time to time with the honey-margarine mixture
	(serves 4–6)

ISRAELI SOUTHERN FRIED CHICKEN, YOU-ALL

2 fryers, dismembered	brush the chicken parts with a mixture of lemon and honey
juice of 1 lemon	
1 tablespoon honey	mix the flour, paprika, and seasonings. roll the chicken parts in this mixture, and shake off excess flour
½ cup flour	
dash paprika	dip the floured chicken parts in beaten egg, then in breadcrumbs, and fry in hot olive oil until golden on all sides. reduce the heat and cook until done inside and crisp outside
½ teaspoon salt	
½ teaspoon pepper	
dash cayenne	
2 eggs, beaten	(serves 6)
1 cup breadcrumbs	
olive oil	

162

MAGUINA *(Baked Beef)*

1 pound beef, thinly sliced	sauté the beef slices, onions, and garlic in hot olive oil for 10 minutes, using a heavy skillet
2 onions, chopped	
1 clove garlic, minced	
3 tablespoons olive oil	add the tomato paste, mushrooms, potatoes, and seasonings and continue cooking, stirring, until potatoes are done, and remove from heat
½ cup tomato paste	
1 cup sliced mushrooms	
2 large potatoes, peeled and thinly sliced	grease a baking dish, pour in the skillet contents, and add the beaten eggs. mix well and bake in a preheated 350° oven for about a half hour
½ teaspoon salt	
dash paprika	(serves 4–6)
dash nutmeg	
dash cinnamon	
8 eggs, beaten	

163

CARNATZLACH (*Meat Balls*)

1½ pounds finely chopped lean beef (chuck is best)	mix all the ingredients thoroughly and form into small croquettes
1 clove garlic, crushed	
1 onion, finely chopped	pan-broil in a little oil, using a heavy skillet, until golden brown
2 eggs, beaten	
1 teaspoon salt	(serves 4)
pepper	
dash cayenne	
olive oil	

KIRSEH (*Yemenite Tripe*)

1 pound tripe, cut into small squares	wash the tripe and bring to a quick boil in salted water. turn the heat down to a simmer
2 cups water	
2 teaspoons salt	cook the onion, garlic, and tomato in the oil for a minute or so and add to the tripe
1 onion, chopped	
2 cloves garlic, crushed	season, cover and simmer slowly for an hour or so (or until tripe is tender)
1 tomato, chopped (or a couple tablespoons tomato paste)	(serves 4)
3 tablespoons olive oil (or other cooking oil)	
dash each of cayenne, pepper, cumin, coriander, cardamom	

164

NOAH'S PUDDING

10 tablespoons rice	wash the rice and chick-peas and soak overnight
4 tablespoons chick-peas	
water	strain, place in a large pot, cover with water, and cook until the mixture becomes mushy (about 4 hours)
2 cups milk	
1 cup sugar	strain, add the milk, sugar, honey, and fruit and cook again until fruit is soft and mixture is thick
½ cup honey	
½ cup dried apricots, chopped	remove from heat, stir in the nuts, cool, and serve
½ cup dried raisins	
½ cup dried figs, chopped	(serves about 6)
2 cups sliced nuts (almonds, walnuts, pine nuts, etc.)	

TEHAINIM MITUKIM (*Sweet Figs*)

2 cups water	boil the water, add the honey or sugar, make a syrup, and add the spices
½ cup honey (or 1 cup sugar)	
pinch ginger	add the figs and simmer gently until syrup is thick
pinch cinnamon	
1 pound figs (fresh or dried)	remove from the heat, sprinkle with grated orange and lemon peel and nuts. serve cold
1 tablespoon grated orange peel	
1 tablespoon grated lemon peel	(serves 4)
2 tablespoons pine nuts	

165

11

WHO
NEEDS
AN
AMERICAN
COOKBOOK

WHO NEEDS AN AMERICAN COOKBOOK

SHE-CRAB SOUP

NEW ORLEANS GUMBO

NEW ENGLAND CLAM CHOWDER

MANHATTAN CLAM CHOWDER

CHARLESTON FISH CHOWDER

PHILADELPHIA PEPPER POT

SHAKER PEASE PORRIDGE

SOUTHERN BAKED MACARONI

MARYLAND CRAB IMPERIAL

KANSAS CATFISH SAUTÉ

OYSTERS ROCKEFELLER

HAWAIIAN BARBECUED HAM

HAWAIIAN CHICKEN

SOUTHERN FRIED CHICKEN

ANN SERANNE'S RIB ROAST OF BEEF

NEW ENGLAND BOILED DINNER

BRUNSWICK STEW

GOOD OLD AMERICAN HASH

OLD VIRGINIA SPOON BREAD

168 JOHNNY CAKE

HUSH PUPPIES

HASTY PUDDING

SALLY LUNN

MONTANA SOURDOUGH BREAD

BROWN BETTY

PENNSYLVANIA DUTCH SHOO-FLY PIE

To several parts of New England add a generous portion of the Middle Atlantic and the South, stir in the Old West and the Pacific Coast, and flavor generously with France, Italy, Germany, Mexico, and the rest of the world. (serves 200,000,000)

And that's the recipe for American cooking.

Who needs a cookbook.

Some of the regional favorites that have made America's cooking what it is today—unpredictable, variable, delectable—are set down in this all-too-short chapter so that you can take something of a nationwide cook's tour without leaving your kitchen.

SHE-CRAB SOUP

Here is a soup from the old South, where great attention has always been paid to the female. In the case of this recipe, the female is more delicate than the male because the eggs are so good, but He-crab Soup is not to be sneered at, either.

1 tablespoon butter	melt the butter in the top of a double boiler, blend with flour, and pour in the milk gradually, stirring
1 tablespoon flour	
1 quart milk	
2 cups crabmeat (with the eggs)	add the crabmeat, onion, and seasonings and simmer slowly for about 20 minutes
1 slice onion, grated	serve with a teaspoon sherry in each bowl and top with whipped cream, parsley, and paprika
dash Worcestershire	
pinch mace	
salt	(serves 4–6)
pepper	
sherry	
whipped cream	
chopped parsley	
paprika	

169

NEW ORLEANS GUMBO

4 slices bacon, and 2 slices ham, (or a 1-inch cube salt pork), chopped	sauté the bacon and ham (or salt pork) until brown in a porcelain pan. remove from pan and set aside
1 onion, chopped	add onion, garlic, pepper, celery and sauté about 10 minutes
1 clove garlic, crushed	
½ green pepper, chopped	
1 stalk celery with leaves, chopped	add tomatoes, okra, seasonings, and 4 cups boiling water. (Note: Okra turns black unless cooked in porcelain)
1 large can tomatoes, chopped	
2 cups canned okra	simmer about an hour. just before serving drop in the filé and stir like mad
pinch thyme	
1 bay leaf	serve both the bacon, ham (or pork) bits added to each bowl
dash Tabasco	
salt	(serves 4–6)
pepper	
4 cups boiling water	
2 teaspoons filé	

170

To this Gumbo base you can add (5 minutes before serving) oysters, crab, cooked shrimp, cooked chicken, or a combination of any of them.

NEW ENGLAND CLAM CHOWDER

1-inch cube salt pork, diced	cook the salt pork in a pot until the fat melts and set aside the crisp bits
1 onion, finely chopped	
2 cups cubed potatoes	add the onion and sauté until golden
1½ pints shelled hard clams, chopped (any kind, but the largest are the toughest) or use canned clams	add the potatoes and clams (save the juice), dredge with a little flour, and pour in a cup of boiling water
flour	simmer until potatoes are tender (about 20 minutes) and add the milk and 3 tablespoons butter
1 cup boiling water	
3 cups hot milk	
4 tablespoons butter	thicken the clam juice with a tablespoon flour and a tablespoon butter, and stir into the chowder
salt	
pepper	season to taste and serve with some of the crisp pork bits in each bowl
	(serves 6)

MANHATTAN CLAM CHOWDER

171

Make New England Clam Chowder, substituting water for milk and adding 2 cups drained canned tomatoes and ¼ teaspoon dried thyme.

CHARLESTON FISH CHOWDER

Make New England Clam Chowder, substituting a pound of some kind of fish (cut into small pieces) for the clams and fish stock or clam broth for the milk. Season with a little cayenne pepper and nutmeg or allspice and add a tablespoon catsup. Then toss in 2 jiggers of dry sherry.

PHILADELPHIA PEPPER POT

2 tablespoons butter

1 onion, chopped

1 stalk celery, chopped

½ green pepper, chopped

1 cup chopped potato

2 tablespoons flour

3 cups chicken broth

½ pound cooked honeycomb tripe, cut into ½-inch squares

salt

pepper

½ cup light cream

sauté the onion, celery, pepper, and potato in the butter until brown, using a large saucepan

stir in the flour and then the chicken broth and tripe

season, cover and simmer for an hour

add the cream, stir, and serve

(serves 4–6)

172

SHAKER PEASE PORRIDGE

1 cup split peas

1 quart chicken or beef bouillon

1 tablespoon Worcestershire

1 onion, chopped

1 carrot, chopped

1 stalk celery, chopped

salt

pepper

croutons

simmer the peas in the bouillon for a couple of hours, using a large pot

add the other ingredients and cook half an hour longer

put through a sieve, reheat, and serve with croutons

(serves 4–6)

SOUTHERN BAKED MACARONI

½ pound macaroni

salt

water

1 tablespoon butter

1 egg, beaten

1 teaspoon salt

1 teaspoon pepper

2 cups grated cheese

½ cup milk

cook the macaroni in salted water until tender. drain

stir in the butter and egg, add the seasonings, cheese, and milk

stir and transfer to a buttered baking dish and bake in a preheated oven at 350° about half an hour or until cheese is melted and dish is brown on top

(serves 4)

173

MARYLAND CRAB IMPERIAL

4 crabs	boil the crabs, remove the meat, save the shells (or use fresh refrigerated lump or back fin crab)
½ onion, chopped	
2 tablespoons butter	
	sauté the onion in the butter, add the crab meat, and season with salt and cayenne. add Worcestershire, English mustard, chive, green pepper, and cream
salt	
cayenne pepper	
dash Worcestershire	
1 teaspoon English mustard	mix well, bind with egg yolk, pile into the shells, and sprinkle with breadcrumbs
1 teaspoon chopped chive	
2 tablespoons chopped green pepper	dot with butter and brown in the oven
2 cups heavy cream	(serves 4)
the yolks of 2 eggs	
breadcrumbs	
butter	

174

KANSAS CATFISH SAUTÉ

Skin and clean the catfish, dredge in a mixture of ½ cup flour and ½ cup cornmeal seasoned with salt and pepper. Fry until tender and golden in a small amount of hot fat.

OYSTERS ROCKEFELLER

12 oysters on the half shell	remove the oysters from their shells
1½ cups sour cream	
1 clove garlic, crushed	mix ½ cup of sour cream with the garlic and put a little of the mixture in each shell
1 cup cooked spinach, finely chopped	place the oysters on the mixture
salt and pepper	
2 tablespoons crumbled crisp bacon	mix the chopped spinach with the rest of the sour cream, a little garlic, salt and pepper, and place a dab on each oyster. top with bacon
breadcrumbs	
2 tablespoons butter	sprinkle with breadcrumbs, dot with butter, and brown under the broiler about 5 minutes
	(serves 2–3, or live a little and eat them all yourself, even if you're not Rockefeller)

HAWAIIAN BARBECUED HAM

175

8 slices boiled ham	brown the ham slightly in the butter, using a heavy skillet. remove ham to a hot platter
2 tablespoons butter	
1 tablespoon vinegar	add the vinegar, mustard, pineapple, salt and pepper. simmer a minute or so and pour over the ham
¼ teaspoon dry mustard	
½ can crushed pineapple	(serves 4)
salt	
pepper	

HAWAIIAN CHICKEN

2 young chickens, cut into pieces

chicken bouillon

2 cups chopped spinach

the meat of 1 coconut, grated

½ pint milk

salt

pepper

put the chicken in a heavy pot, cover with bouillon, and simmer until tender

add the spinach and cook a few minutes longer

meanwhile, slowly heat the grated coconut in milk, drain off the liquid, squeeze out the meat in a cheesecloth bag. discard the pulp—save the liquid

add this coconut milk to the chicken, bring to a boil, season to taste, and serve on rice

(serves 4)

SOUTHERN FRIED CHICKEN

2 cups flour

3 teaspoons baking powder

2 eggs, well beaten

½ cup milk

½ teaspoon salt

pepper

2 young chickens, cut into pieces

cooking fat

milk

cream

salt

mix the flour, baking powder, eggs, milk, and seasonings together, forming a batter

dip the chicken pieces one at a time into the batter and fry in hot fat 1½ to 2 inches deep, using a heavy skillet

serve with cream gravy made by adding half milk and half cream and salt to the skillet and scraping up the crusted juices

(serves 4–6)

177

ANN SERANNE'S RIB ROAST OF BEEF

Remove the short ribs from a 1-rib, 2-rib, 3-rib, or 4-rib roast of beef.

Keep it at room temperature for at least 2½ hours before cooking, place it in an open shallow roasting pan fat side up, and sprinkle with a little flour; season with salt and freshly ground pepper.

Slide the pan into a preheated oven at 500°, cook for 15 minutes per rib, and turn off the oven.

Allow the roast to remain in the oven without opening the door until oven is lukewarm, or about 2 hours.

Roast will have a crunchy brown outside and an internal heat that will be suitable for serving up to four hours. (Serves 2 per rib.)

(Craig Claiborne of *The New York Times* reports that this recipe received the greatest reader response recently. Who needs a cookbook.)

NEW ENGLAND BOILED DINNER

4 pounds corned beef	wash and drain the beef and if very salty soak for half an hour
1 small cabbage, quartered	
3 carrots, sliced	put the meat in boiling water and cook 3–4 hours or until tender
2 small turnips, quartered	
6 potatoes, peeled and halved	an hour before serving add the cabbage, carrots, and turnips
6 small parsnips	
6 medium white onions, peeled	half an hour before serving add the potatoes, parsnips, and onions
	serve very hot on a large platter
	(serves lots)

178

BRUNSWICK STEW

1 4-pound stewing chicken	place the chicken in a heavy pot with the water, bacon, and onion and cook for about an hour or until chicken is tender
1 quart water	
4 slices bacon, cut into pieces	
1 onion, sliced	debone the chicken, cut into small pieces, and return to the pot
2 cups chopped tomatoes	
2 cups diced potatoes	add the tomatoes, potatoes, and lima beans. 10 minutes later add the corn and seasonings. simmer until vegetables are tender
1 cup frozen lima beans	
1 cup frozen or fresh corn kernels	
dash Tabasco sauce	stir in the breadcrumbs and serve
salt	(serves 4–6)
½ cup breadcrumbs	

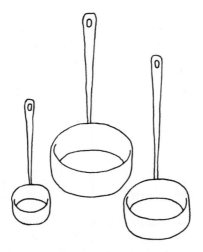

179

GOOD OLD AMERICAN HASH

leftover cooked beef, veal, lamb, chicken, iguana, buffalo, or what have you	grind or chop the meat
	mix meat together with the chopped vegetables
chopped potatoes, onion, hard-cooked eggs, green peppers, parsley, carrots, peas, or what have you	melt butter in a pot, add a little flour, and stir in some of the water or stock
butter	add the meat, vegetables, a little tomato paste, and salt
flour	and pepper
hot water or beef or chicken stock	cook for about 25 minutes, stirring. add as much liquid as you want
tomato paste	
salt	
pepper	

OLD VIRGINIA SPOON BREAD

180

1 cup water-ground white cornmeal	scald the cornmeal with the boiling water and stir in the butter, salt, and egg
1 cup boiling water	
1 tablespoon butter	add the baking powder and milk
1 teaspoon salt	put into a well-buttered pan and bake in a preheated oven at 375° for 40 minutes
1 egg, well beaten	
1½ teaspoons baking powder	serve hot with butter
1 cup milk	(serves 8)

JOHNNY CAKE

1 cup cornmeal	mix all the ingredients in a saucepan. cook, stirring until mixture thickens
2 cups water	
½ teaspoon salt	cool and form into 4 rectangular cakes
1 tablespoon butter	
	bake in a greased pan in a preheated 400° oven for half an hour
	(serves 4)

HUSH PUPPIES

2 cups cornmeal	mix all the ingredients together and form into finger-shaped cakes
2 teaspoons baking powder	
1 teaspoon salt	fry quickly in hot bacon or ham fat and throw them to your noisy little puppies, or eat them yourself
1 small onion, minced	
1 egg, beaten	
½ cup milk	
bacon or ham fat	

181

HASTY PUDDING

1½ cups cornmeal	mix the cornmeal with 1 cup cold water
4 cups water	
½ teaspoon salt	in a heavy saucepan bring the remaining water to a boil and add the salt
powdered sugar	
	slowly and gradually stir in the cold cornmeal mixture, cook over low heat, stirring frequently, for an hour (how hasty can you be) or until mixture is very thick
	serve with powdered sugar
	(serves 4)

SALLY LUNN

2 teaspoons baking powder	mix the baking powder, flour, and salt and add with the milk to the beaten eggs
2 cups flour	
½ teaspoon salt	add the melted butter and mix well
¾ cup milk	
2 eggs, beaten	bake in a well-greased square pan in a preheated 350° oven for about 40 minutes
1 tablespoon butter, melted	
	cut into squares and serve hot
	(serves 8)

182

MONTANA SOURDOUGH BREAD

First you make the "starter." And here is how you do it:

Dissolve an envelope of yeast in half a cup of warm water and let it stand for 5 or 10 minutes.

Put this yeast mixture into a large crock, stir in a couple more cups warm water, 2 cups flour, a tablespoon sugar, and 2 teaspoons salt.

Cover the crock with a towel and let it stand for 3 or 4 days in a warm room, stirring every day.

You will now have produced 4 times as much dough as you started out with and you can keep it that way for the rest of your life—or longer. All you have to do is replace the dough you use with an equal amount of flour-water mixture.

To make Sourdough Bread, add a tablespoon melted butter to 2 cups of the "starter" and mix in ½ teaspoon baking soda, a teaspoon sugar, and enough flour to make a thick dough.

Knead on a floured board until smooth, working in more flour to keep the dough from becoming sticky. Put it into a greased bowl in a warm place and let it rise until almost double and form into a loaf.

The loaf goes into a greased tin and rises again to double its width. It is then baked in a preheated oven at 350° for half an hour or until brown.

183

BROWN BETTY

3 cups applesauce	butter a 1-quart baking dish, spread 1 cup applesauce over bottom of dish
3 tablespoons melted butter	
1½ cups fine breadcrumbs	sprinkle ½ cup breadcrumbs and a tablespoon of melted butter on top and then 1 tablespoon of the sugar-cinnamon mixture
3 tablespoons brown sugar mixed with ½ teaspoon cinnamon and ¼ teaspoon salt	
	repeat until there are 3 layers
cream	bake in a preheated oven at 350° for 25 minutes or until crumbs are golden. serve with hot cream
	(serves 4–6)

184

PENNSYLVANIA DUTCH SHOO-FLY PIE

1 package prepared piecrust

½ cup molasses

½ cup water

2 cups flour

2 tablespoons butter

2 tablespoons lard

¼ teaspoon salt

1 cup sugar

¼ teaspoon cream of tartar

½ teaspoon baking soda

cinnamon

dissolve the molasses in the water and pour into a pie pan lined with piecrust

mix all the other ingredients together and form into crumbs

spread these crumbs evenly on top, sprinkle with cinnamon, and bake in a preheated 350° oven until firm in the center and brown on top

185

12

...OR
ANY
OTHER
KIND
OF
COOKBOOK

AALSOEP (*Eel Soup, Holland*)

SNERT (*Green Pea Soup, Holland*)

BORSCHT (*Russia*)

SOUPA AVGOLEMONO (*Lemon Soup, Greece*)

FONDUE NEUCHÂTEL (*Switzerland*)

FONDUE BOURGUIGNONNE (*Switzerland*)

CHOW FAN (*Fried Rice, China*)

TIEM-SHOON GEE-YOKE (*Sweet and Sour Pork, China*)

SHU PE-GOOD (*Barbecued Spareribs, China*)

BEEF STROGANOFF (*Russia*)

SHASHLIK (*Meat on Skewers, Russia*)

SHISH KEBAB (*Meat on Skewers, Armenian*)

ARNI SOUVLA (*Meat on Skewers, Greece*)

STIFATHO (*Beef Stew, Greece*)

ADJHEM PILAF (*Mutton Pilaf, Greece*)

COUSCOUS (*Morocco, Algeria*)

188

AALSOEP (*Eel Soup, Holland*)

Very famous in Holland—very easy to make.

½ pound eel, cleaned, skinned, and cut into small pieces	boil the eel pieces in salted water until tender, remove, and set aside
3 pints water	add the capers and parsley and bring to a boil
salt	thicken with the butter-flour mixture, simmer for 15 minutes, and strain
4 tablespoons capers	
1 small bunch parsley	
3 tablespoons butter	add the pieces of eel and serve
3 tablespoons flour	(serves 4)

SNERT (*Green Pea Soup, Holland*)

1 pound fresh pig's hock	boil the pig's hock in the water about an hour or until tender, skimming the scum as it rises to the surface
2 quarts water	
1 pound split green peas	remove the hock and set aside
the white parts of 2 leeks, chopped	add the peas to the liquid and simmer for half an hour, then add the remaining ingredients and continue simmering for half an hour longer
2 stalks celery, chopped	
2 onions, chopped	
2 teaspoons salt	remove the meat from the hock, dice, and add to the soup
1 teaspoon freshly ground pepper	(serves 6–8)

189

BORSCHT (*Russia*)

If you have a few beets on hand, you can't go wrong with this wonderful Slavic soup. (You can't even spell it wrong—borsch, borscht, borsht, bortsch, bortch.) Here's the recipe: Take some meat and some vegetables (beets are a must) and cook them with some water or stock, season, and eat. If you think you need a little more specific guidance, let these directions—and your conscience—be your guide:

1 pound lean meat, cubed (beef and/or pork and/or veal and/or chicken)

put the meat into salted water, cover and simmer about an hour or until tender. drain, and set aside

1 quart water or some kind of stock

1 teaspoon salt

to the stock add the vegetables, vinegar, and butter. season with a little pepper, cover, and simmer for about a half hour

2 cups chopped raw beets

2 cups chopped carrots, turnips, green beans, or what have you

add the meat, simmer 15 minutes longer, check the seasonings, stir in the sour cream and serve

(serves 4–6)

1 onion, chopped

1 small head cabbage, shredded

190

2 tablespoons tomato puree

2 tablespoons vinegar

1 tablespoon butter

pepper

½ cup sour cream

SOUPA AVGOLEMONO (Lemon Soup, Greece)

4 cups chicken stock	cook the rice and stock for 10 minutes or till the rice
2 tablespoons rice	is soft
2 egg yolks	add a little of the stock to the egg yolks and mix in the
juice of 1 large lemon	lemon juice. stir and add to the stock, season to taste, and
salt	serve with croutons
pepper	

FONDUE NEUCHÂTEL (Switzerland)

This is a sort of Swiss rarebit—with a kick. Served in a chafing dish, kept hot by a spirit flame, the fondue sits in the middle of the table, and is shared by one and all in a most informal manner. The diners, armed with long two-pronged forks, spear a hunk of bread and dunk. A great deal of wine is often consumed during the process.

4 cups grated Gruyère or Swiss cheese	rub the inside of a chafing dish with cut garlic
2 cups dry white wine	pour in the wine, heat, and add the cheese and stir until
1 clove garlic, cut	cheese is melted
2 teaspoons potato flour or cornstarch	mix the flour and kirsch and add gradually to the cheese, stirring. season with nutmeg
¼ cup kirsch (or very dry sherry)	and salt. keep hot. serve with hunks of French bread
¼ teaspoon nutmeg	(serves 4–6)
salt	

191

FONDUE BOURGUIGNONNE (*Switzerland*)

This is another social Swiss dish. Hot oil replaces the cheese mixture and cubes of tender, raw beef are speared instead of bread. The meat is dipped into the sizzling oil and browned, and then dunked into a choice of sauces, placed in individual dishes.

Two pounds of very tender beef, preferably tenderloin, cut into 1-inch cubes, will serve four. Two cups peanut oil combined with two cups butter are heated in a metal or earthenware pot over a spirit lamp or Sterno. Sauce suggestions: curry, mustard, horseradish, béarnaise, barbecue, Epicurean, or any of the prepared steak sauces. Or try some of the following butters: anchovy butter, garlic butter, Roquefort butter, tomato butter . . .

CHOW FAN (*Fried Rice, Chinese*)

6 tablespoons peanut oil or other cooking oil

heat the oil in a heavy skillet and scramble the eggs until firm

2 eggs, beaten

2 cups canned bean sprouts

add the bean sprouts, onions, monosodium, and soy sauce and simmer 2 minutes longer

1 cup chopped onions

2 teaspoons monosodium glutamate

add the rice and scallions, stir, and simmer for 5 minutes

192

6 teaspoons soy sauce

(serves 6)

10 cups cold cooked rice

½ cup scallions, finely chopped

TIEM-SHOON GEE-YOKE
(Sweet and Sour Pork, China)

2 teaspoons soy sauce

½ teaspoon monosodium glutamate

½ teaspoon ginger

2 tablespoons dry sherry wine

2 pounds fresh pork, cut into 1-inch cubes

4 eggs, beaten

½ cup flour

3 tablespoons cornstarch

4 tablespoons peanut oil (or other cooking oil)

1 cup sugar dissolved in 1 cup hot water

1 cup vinegar

1 cup sweet pickle, diced

2 green peppers, sliced

1 tomato, diced

1 cup canned pineapple, cubed

mix 1 teaspoon soy sauce with the monosodium, ginger, and sherry and marinate the pork for 10 or 15 minutes

remove the pork and dip into a batter made by mixing the eggs, flour, and half of the cornstarch together

fry the pork in hot oil until golden on all sides

mix the sugar-water, vinegar, pickle, peppers, tomato, and pineapple together. thicken with the remaining cornstarch and simmer for 2 minutes

add the fried pork and cook until gravy thickens

(serves 4)

193

SHU PE-GOOD (*Barbecued Spareribs, China*)

2 pounds fresh pork spareribs, separated

6 tablespoons soy sauce

1 tablespoon honey

1 tablespoon sugar

2 tablespoons applesauce

1 teaspoon Worcestershire sauce

2 cloves garlic, crushed

2 teaspoons monosodium glutamate

mix the soy sauce, honey, sugar, applesauce, Worcestershire, garlic, and monosodium glutamate

cover spareribs well with this mixture and marinate for a couple of hours

grill under a hot broiler until brown on all sides and serve with canned duck sauce and English mustard

BEEF STROGANOFF (*Russia*)

194

1 pound beef fillet, sirloin or porterhouse, cut into 1-inch squares ½ inch thick

salt

freshly ground pepper

2 tablespoons butter

½ onion, chopped

1 tablespoon flour

1 cup beef stock or consommé

1 teaspoon prepared mustard

2 tablespoons sour cream

season the beef slices with salt and pepper, and brown them in a heavy skillet with a tablespoon of butter and the chopped onion. remove the beef

add the remaining butter and the flour, brown, and then pour in the stock, add the mustard, and blend until smooth

stir in the sour cream, replace the beef slices, simmer about 10 minutes, and serve

(serves 4)

SHASHLIK (*Russia*)
SHISH KEBAB (*Armenia*)
ARNI SOUVLA (*Greece*)

To the Russians it's *Shashlik*, to the Armenians it's *Shish Kebab*, to the Greeks it's *Arni Souvla*. Pronounce it as you will, with some variations it always ends up as skewered lamb.

1 small leg of lamb, trimmed and cut into 2-inch cubes	place the meat in a shallow dish, cover with a marinade made by mixing the oil, wine, vinegar, garlic, salt and pepper
¼ cup olive oil	
½ cup red wine	cover and marinate overnight, stirring occasionally
¼ cup vinegar	
2 cloves garlic, crushed	string the meat on a skewer and grill over white-hot charcoal coals or under broiler for 5 minutes on each side, basting with the marinade
2 teaspoons salt	
pepper	

Meat cubes can be alternated on the skewer with cubes of egg-plant, tomato wedges, small white onions, slices of green peppers, or mushroom caps.

195

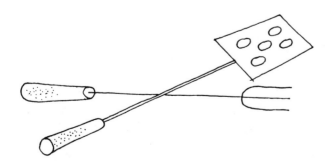

STIFATHO (*Beef Stew, Greece*)

2 pounds lean beef, cut into 2-inch cubes

if the meat is not tender, marinate it overnight in the wine

½ cup dry red wine

in a heavy skillet brown the meat in the oil and add the butter, tomato puree, vinegar, water, and spices

½ cup olive oil

½ cup butter

½ cup tomato puree

bring to a boil, reduce the heat, cover and simmer for about an hour or until meat is tender

1 tablespoon vinegar

2 cups water

1 cinnamon stick

brown the onions slightly, add to the casserole and cook about 15 minutes longer

pinch saffron

(serves 4–6)

salt

pepper

6 small white onions

196

ADJHEM PILAF *(Mutton Pilaf, Greece)*

1 cup raw rice (long-grain type)

2 tablespoons butter

½ pound mutton or lamb, sliced

1 tablespoon olive oil

1 pint beef or chicken broth

salt

pepper

melt the butter and sauté the rice for 5 to 8 minutes or until golden

in a separate skillet brown the sliced meat in the oil

combine the meat and rice, add the stock, season with salt and pepper, and simmer until all the liquid has been absorbed and the mixture is just moist

(serves 4)

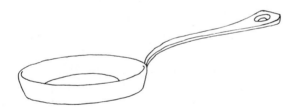

197

COUSCOUS (*Morocco, Algeria, etc.*)

One of the most popular dishes of North Africa and the Middle East, Couscous is made from millet or semolina, a large, hard wheat grain (available at most Middle East stores).

To prepare Couscous the way the natives do is a little tricky and requires some very special equipment consisting of a glazed earthenware marmite and a sort of strainer (also of earthenware) that fits over it.

Into the bottom pot you put a stew of mutton, lamb, or chicken and onions (all previously browned). You can also include some carrots, pimientos, beans, or almost any kind of vegetables. Or you can fill the bottom pot simply with some kind of dried beans that have been soaked overnight.

Into the top strainer goes the semolina, but not until it has been given a triple treatment with boiling water to make the grains swell.

Now the bottom marmite with the stew or beans goes onto the stove (usually charcoal) and is covered with a damp cloth to prevent the steam from escaping at the sides. The strainer marmite containing the swollen grains fits over the top.

After three hours or so the meat is stewed and the semolina is steamed. Couscous is served on a hot platter—the stew in the center surrounded by the semolina.

198

13

COFFEES
AND
TEAS

CAFÉ BRÛLOT (*France*)

COFFEE CARIOCA (*Puerto Rico*)

CAFÉ CHANTILLY (*France*)

IRISH COFFEE (*Ireland*)

GROG (*United States*)

CAFÉ ORLÉANS FLAMBÉ (*France*)

CAFFE BORGIA (*Italy*)

CAFFE CAPPUCCINO (*Italy*)

CAFFE CIOCOLACCINO (*Italy*)

COWBOY CHUCK-WAGON COFFEE (*United States*)

TEA

200

CAFÉ BRÛLOT (*France*)

8 lumps sugar	place sugar, cloves, and cinnamon into a chafing dish or other suitable container
4 whole cloves	
1 cinnamon stick	add lemon peel and orange peel
1 lemon peel, cut into a spiral	
1 orange peel, cut into a spiral	add cognac, set over flame, and heat, stirring constantly
½ cup cognac	ignite cognac, continuing to stir
2 cups very hot, extra-strong coffee	after about a minute, slowly pour in the hot coffee, stirring
	ladle into demitasse cups while still flaming (do not serve the spices or peels) and serve at once
	(serves 4)

COFFEE CARIOCA (*Puerto Rico*)

2 tablespoons sugar	place the sugar, orange peel, and coffee in a heatproof bowl
1 orange peel, sliced	
¼ cup coffee, ground fine	stir in boiling water and let stand for half an hour
2 cups boiling water	strain into coffeepot and heat to just under boiling
½ cup dark rum	stir in rum, pour into demitasse cups, and serve topped with whipped cream and a little grated orange peel
¼ cup sweetened whipped cream	
	(serves 4)

201

CAFÉ CHANTILLY (*France*)

To a demitasse of hot coffee add 1 tablespoon cognac. Float a teaspoon heavy cream on top.

IRISH COFFEE (*Ireland*)

2 teaspoons sugar	put the sugar and whiskey into a wine glass. fill almost to the top with strong black coffee, stir, and top with cream
1-ounce jigger Irish whiskey	
strong black coffee	
1 tablespoon whipped cream or heavy cream	after six or seven of these, who minds the cold Irish nights

GROG (*United States*)

2 tablespoons butter	cream the butter with the brown sugar, add the spices, and mix thoroughly. this spice base can be kept under refrigeration indefinitely in a covered container
½ pound brown sugar	
pinch each of cinnamon, nutmeg, allspice, cloves, salt	
lemon peel	put a teaspoon of the spice mix into a 6-ounce mug and add a strip of orange peel and lemon peel
orange peel	
light rum	
heavy cream	add 3 tablespoons light rum and 2 tablespoons heavy cream
very hot coffee	fill mug with hot coffee

202

CAFÉ ORLÉANS FLAMBÉ (*France*)

4 tablespoons brown sugar	combine sugar, spices, lemon peel, and hot coffee in a chafing dish or other suitable container
2 whole allspice	
1 cinnamon stick	
1 teaspoon grated lemon peel	heat to just below boiling, stirring
2 cups hot strong coffee	heat cognac in a ladle and ignite
½ cup cognac	
	quickly pour over coffee mixture, stir, and ladle into demitasse cups
	(serves 4)

CAFFE BORGIA (*Italy*)

In a large demitasse combine hot Italian coffee and hot chocolate in equal quantities. Top with sweetened whipped cream and sprinkle with grated orange peel.

CAFFE CAPPUCCINO (*Italy*)

In a large demitasse combine equal quantities of hot Italian coffee and heavy cream. Sprinkle with cinnamon and nutmeg and serve with a lump of sugar.

203

CAFFE CIOCOLACCINO (*Italy*)

Follow recipe for Caffe Cappuccino and top with sweetened whipped cream and chocolate shavings.

COWBOY CHUCK-WAGON COFFEE *(United States)*

2 eggs	wash eggs, break, and beat slightly
2 cups cold water	add 1 cup cold water, egg
dash salt	shells, salt, and coffee
1 cup ground coffee	place in large coffeepot and add boiling water. stir well.
12 cups boiling water	stuff spout with paper to prevent escape of fragrant aroma

set over direct heat, bring slowly to a boil, and boil 3 minutes

remove from direct heat and pour in 1 cup cold water to clear (cold water, being heavier than hot, sinks to bottom of pot carrying grounds with it)

let stand for 10 minutes near fire and serve

(serves 15)

204

TEA

Tea is the principal drink in many parts of the world. In England, especially, it's a necessity of life! Tea for breakfast, tea for lunch, for dinner—and at all the hours in between. You wonder how the English managed before they found out about tea. Yet, incredibly, there once was such a time. September 25, 1661, Samuel Pepys wrote in his diary, "I sent for a cup of tea (a China drink) of which I had never drunk before...." Imagine poor old Pepys wasting away half his life without a cup of tea!

Anybody can make tea. All you have to do is soak leaves in boiling water. The leaves are picked from a shrub called *Camellia sinensis*, grown in China, India, Ceylon, Japan, and other Oriental countries, and subjected to some sort of curing process. The water comes from the cold-water tap in your kitchen. The lift you get when you drink tea comes from the caffeine in the leaves.

If you want to make *good* tea you have to follow a few pretty important rules. First, you preheat a teapot and dry it. Second, you pour in boiling water made from freshly drawn cold water (stale or reheated water is lacking in air and tastes flat). Third, you add the tea (in England it's most often India tea)—1 teaspoon, or 1 tea bag, per cup. Plus 1. Fourth, let it stand for 3 or 4 or 5 minutes. Fifth, decant or strain into a second (serving) pot that has also been preheated. That's it. If it comes out too strong for you, add a little hot water, but don't judge strength by color. Some dark teas may be delicate in flavor, some light teas strong and robust.

205

14

A
WORD
ABOUT
WINES

Wine is as old as civilization itself. Wherever there is fruit there is fermentation, and usually somebody standing around ready to experiment with it. There is ample evidence that the Chinese experimented as early as four thousand years ago. The Persians and Egyptians appear to have known all about growing grapes and making wine even earlier, perhaps five or six thousand years ago. Then the word began to get around. The Egyptians taught the Greeks, the Greeks taught the Romans, and the Romans taught the French. The French taught the world.

Successful viniculture requires a plentiful supply of good earth, sunshine, rain, and love—four ingredients that seem especially plentiful in France, Italy, and Spain, undeniably the leading wine countries of the world. The relative proportion of these ingredients determines the quality of the wine. It also determines flavor, clarity, and bouquet—qualities that can vary subtly or enormously from vineyard to vineyard over the space of a mere acre—and from season to season.

Wine is the most versatile of beverages. It can be red or white, sweet or dry, still or sparkling; it can be blended, fortified, or spiced. Champagne, for example, is blended from the wines of different vineyards, and sometimes of different years. When the blending wines are all of the same year, the champagne is known as vintage champagne. All true champagnes come from the regions of Rheims and Épernay—formerly the province of Champagne—and are bottled before the fermentation process finishes, producing an effervescence when the cork is popped. Whee!

In one form or another, wine can be consumed at almost any time of the day or year and for almost any reason—to celebrate, to console, to cure, to whet the appetite, to digest the meal.

209

"Wine is the most healthful and hygienic of beverages," said Louis Pasteur, who was in the health business.

"Use a little wine for thy stomach's sake," said Saint Paul—and he didn't mean to bathe in it.

"Wine refreshes the stomach, sharpens the appetite, blunts care and sadness, conduces to slumber," said Pliny. (Except he said it in Latin.)

There's no doubt about it, wine is the most important thing that has happened to man's stomach since food. And its enjoyment plays a great part in the digestion of food. But this enjoyment, by no means absolute, is elusive, inconstant, and often unpredictable. To quote Dr. Stanley Radel, Assistant Professor of Chemistry, The City College of the City University of New York, "The enjoyment of a wine is proportional to the concentration of ethyl alcohol and inversely proportional to the concentration of acetic acid. In physico-chemical parlance we may write

$$\text{ENJOYMENT} = k \times \frac{C_2H_5OH}{CH_3COOH}$$

where the proportionality constant, k, is given by

$$k = \sqrt{\text{CLARITY} \times \text{BOUQUET} \times \text{TASTE}}$$

This constant must be empirically determined for each wine, and is invariably larger for the great wines. In layman terms, k is called the 'character' of the wine.

"The concentration of alcohol generally ranges from 7 to 15 percent for non-fortified wines, and is always stated on the bottle. High acetic acid concentrations result in a sour taste, and such wines are somewhere on the path towards a 'wine vinegar.' It has been claimed [*] that acid concentration in excess of 1/7 of 1 percent can be readily detected, even by beginners."

Great importance is frequently attached to the service of wine with meals—the "right" wine in the "right" glass served in the "right" way at the "right" temperature with the "right" dish—all that sort of thing. It's enough to drive a conscientious host to drink—water.

Relax. Be yourself. But if you're in doubt, follow these simple rules and you can't go wrong—and you'll end up being the best sommelier on your block.

210

1. Serve the wine in a glass (tin cups are out!). Any kind of glass will do. Stemmed glasses let you enjoy the color of the wine while you are sipping and let you drink chilled wine without warming it.

   Wide saucer-type stemmed glasses are most often used for champagne, but the taller, narrower type holds the bubbles longer.

[*] Frank Schoonmaker, *Encyclopedia of Wine* (New York, Hastings House, 1964).

2. Color? Serve what you like. Many people prefer red with red meat, white with light meats, chicken, fish, oysters. Green wine, of course, with the salad.
3. Choose a light wine or a heavy one, a dry wine or a sweet one. Most often sweet wines go better with sweet foods, dry wines with meat, and always with fish.
4. Serve the wine either chilled or at room temperature. Usually white wines taste better chilled—champagnes iced.

A word about wine types. The best-known dinner wines are the Bordeaux and Burgundies of France and those of the Rhone and Loire valleys, from the Rhine banks of Germany, and from the mountains and valleys of Italy. And there are good American wines coming from vineyards fast recovering from the setback of prohibition years.

Here is a far from complete list of some of the best-known names in dinner wines (color and origin of growth are indicated parenthetically):

Anjou (white, rosé—Loire)
Barbera (red—Piedmont)
Bardolino (red—Venetia)
Barsac (white—Bordeaux)
Beaujolais (red—Burgundy)
Beaune (red—Burgundy)
Chablis (white—Burgundy)
Châteauneuf-du-Pape (red—Rhone)
Chianti (red—Tuscany)
Côte Rotie (red—Rhone)
Graves (white, red—Bordeaux)
Hermitage (white, red—Rhone)
Hochheimer (white—Rheingau)
Johannisberger (white—Rheingau)
Liebfraumilch (white—Rheinhausen)
Mâcon (red—Burgundy)
Manzanares (red—Spain)
Mataro (red—Catalonia, Spain)
Médoc (red—Bordeaux)
Meursault (white—Burgundy)
Montrachet (white—Burgundy)

211

Nebbiolo (Piedmont)
Niersteiner (white—Rheinhausen)
Orvieto (white—Umbria)
Pomerol (red—Bordeaux)
Pouilly-Fuissé (white—Burgundy)
Pouilly-Fumé (white—Loire)
Rudesheimer (white—Rheingau)
Saint-Émilion (red—Bordeaux)
Sauterne (white—Bordeaux)
Soave (white—Venetia)
Tusto (red—Alicante, Spain)
Valpolicella (red—Venetia)
Valdepinas (red—Spain)
Vouvray (white—Loire)

And here are a few of the better-known dessert and fortified wines:

Amontillado Sherry (Andalusia, Spain)
Madeira (Madeira)
Manzanilla Sherry (Spain)
Málaga (Spain)
Marsala (Italy)
Oloroso (cream sherry—Spain)
Port (Portugal)
Tio Pepe (dry sherry—Spain)
Tokay (Hungary)

212

INDEX

INDEX

215

C

221

223